New Thinking in Soviet Military Policy

CHATHAM HOUSE PAPERS

General Series Editor: William Wallace
Soviet Foreign Policy Programme Director: Neil Malcolm

The Royal Institute of International Affairs, at Chatham House in London, has provided an impartial forum for discussion and debate on current international issues for some 70 years. Its resident research fellows, specialized information resources, and range of publications, conferences, and meetings span the fields of international politics, economics, and security. The Institute is independent of government.

Chatham House Papers are short monographs on current policy problems which have been commissioned by the RIIA. In preparing the papers, authors are advised by a study group of experts convened by the RIIA, and publication of a paper indicates that the Institute regards it as an authoritative contribution to the public debate. The Institute does not, however, hold opinions of its own; the views expressed in this publication are the responsibility of the author.

CHATHAM HOUSE PAPERS

New Thinking in Soviet Military Policy

Christoph Bluth

The Royal Institute of International Affairs

Pinter Publishers
London

© Royal Institute of International Affairs, 1990

First published in Great Britain in 1990 by
Pinter Publishers Limited
25 Floral Street, London WC2E 9DS

All rights reserved. No part of this publication may be reproduced, stored in a retrieval system, or transmitted by any other means without the prior written permission of the copyright holder. Please direct all inquiries to the publishers.

British Library Cataloguing in Publication Data

A CIP catalogue record for this book is available from the British Library

ISBN 0-86187-880-9 (Paperback)
      0-86187-113-8 (Hardback)

Reproduced from copy supplied by
Stephen Austin and Sons Ltd
Printed and bound in Great Britain by
Biddles Ltd

CONTENTS

Abbreviations/vi
Acknowledgments/viii
1 Introduction/1
2 Soviet military doctrine/9
3 The sources of Soviet security policy/22
4 Strategic arms policy/36
5 Soviet strategic defence/50
6 Theatre nuclear weapons/65
7 Conventional force planning/80
8 The future of East-West relations/100
Notes/105

ABBREVIATIONS

ABM	Anti-Ballistic Missile
ALCM	Air-Launched Cruise Missile
ASAT	Antisatellite
ASW	Anti-Submarine Warfare
ATBM	Anti-Tactical Ballistic Missile
BMD	Ballistic Missile Defence
CC	Central Committee
CDE	Conference on Confidence- and Security-Building Measures and Disarmament in Europe
CDU	Christian Democratic Union (West Germany)
CEP	Circular Error Probable
CFE	Conventional Forces in Europe
CPSU	Communist Party of the Soviet Union
CSCE	Conference on Security and Cooperation in Europe
CSU	Christian Social Union (West Germany)
FOFA	Follow-On-Forces-Attack
GLCM	Ground-Launched Cruise Missile
ICBM	Intercontinental Ballistic Missile
IMEMO	Institute of World Economy and International Relations
IMRD	Institute of the International Labour Movement
INF	Intermediate Nuclear Forces
IRBM	Intermediate-Range Ballistic Missile
ISKAN	Institute of the United States and Canada
KGB	Committee for State Security
LPAR	Large Phased-Array Radar
LRTNF	Long-Range Theatre Nuclear Forces

Abbreviations

LTDP	Long-Term Defence Programme
MBFR	Mutual and Balanced Force Reductions
MFA	Ministry of Foreign Affairs (Soviet Union)
MIRV	Multiple Independently-targetable Re-entry Vehicle
MLRS	Multiple Launch Rocket System
MPA	Main Political Administration
MX	Missile Experimental
OMG	Operational Manoeuvre Group
PVO	Anti-Air Defence
SALT	Strategic Arms Limitation Talks
SAM	Surface-to-Air Missile
SDI	Strategic Defence Initiative
SLBM	Submarine-Launched Ballistic Missile
SLCM	Submarine-Launched Cruise Missile
SNF	Short-Range Nuclear Forces
SRAM	Short-Range Attack Missile
SRINF	Short-Range Intermediate Nuclear Forces
SS	Surface-to-Surface (Soviet missile)
START	Strategic Arms Reduction Talks
TNF	Theatre Nuclear Forces
VPK	Military-Industrial Commission (Soviet Union)

ACKNOWLEDGMENTS

Many people have given help and advice during the writing of this paper. First of all, I wish to thank Alex Pravda for inviting me to write it. A number of people have generously shared their expertise with me while I was engaged in research. Among them are Hannes Adomeit, Roy Allison, Oleg Amirov, Sergei Blagovolin, Christopher Davis, Lawrence Freedman, Raymond L. Garthoff, David Holloway, Aleksei Izyumov, Sergei Karaganov, Gennady Kolosov, Stephen Meyer, Michael MccGwire and Stephen Shenfield. The staff at the Royal Institute of International Affairs, in particular Neil Malcolm, John Roper and Pauline Wickham, deserve my gratitude. The members of the RIIA study group which discussed the paper contributed fruitful ideas and criticisms. I also wish to thank IMEMO for inviting me for a study visit to further the research. The advice, encouragement and friendship of Michael Dasaro, Adrian Hyde-Price, Elaine Holoboff, Vladimir Kapustin, Martin Navias, Vladimir Salov, Yury Usachev and Helen E. Webb played a crucial role. My wife, Alison Williams-Bluth, provided the loving emotional and intellectual support without which the book could not have been written. It is dedicated to her.

This study is published under the auspices of the Soviet foreign policy programme funded by the ESRC (grant no. E 00 22 2011).

April 1990   C.B.

1
INTRODUCTION

Since the end of World War II, the global confrontation between East and West has been a central feature of international relations. One of the key aspects of this confrontation has been the growth in Soviet and US military power. During the Cold War the Soviet Union and the United States came to be opponents facing each other in a monumental global power-struggle which threatened to plunge the world into a nuclear holocaust. One focus of the military confrontation was Central Europe, where both sides have built up a large concentration of conventional and nuclear forces. A large scholarly literature has been devoted to the examination of the causes of the Cold War and the dynamics of the military competition which accompanied it. In so far as military policy is determined by foreign policy objectives, the nature of Soviet foreign policy has been a central issue. The early postwar Western literature on Soviet foreign policy is characterized by a remarkable degree of unanimity on the objectives of Soviet foreign policy. Daniel Yergin describes this consensus as 'an image of the Soviet Union as a world revolutionary state, denying the possibilities of coexistence, committed to unrelenting ideological warfare, powered by a messianic drive for world mastery.'[1]

Not all specialists in Soviet foreign policy would have expressed it in those terms. For example, while many experts may have surmised that the policy of 'coexistence' was merely a ruse, others argued that it was none the less an element of declared Soviet policy which was progressively filled with greater substance. However, although a

Introduction

diversity in the interpretation of Soviet foreign policy objectives was already developing, the dominant view was that the Soviet Union was fundamentally expansionist and therefore that Soviet military power represented a serious threat to the West. The Soviet state was described as a totalitarian structure under effective central control by a leadership that allowed no deviation from the prescribed path. Every action in foreign and military policy could be interpreted as a tactical step designed to further the general goals based on a calculation of the correlation of forces.

The other view of the Soviet Union 'downplayed the role of ideology and the foreign policy consequences of authoritarian domestic practices, and instead saw the Soviet Union behaving like a traditional Great Power within the international system, rather than trying to overthrow it.'[2]

The empirical evidence for both these interpretations was ambiguous. In the early postwar years the Soviet Union was concerned to consolidate its hold over Eastern Europe, a policy which then was viewed by the Western powers as a form of aggression,[3] but which has in later years been reinterpreted as an essentially conservative policy arising out of Soviet security concerns in the aftermath of World War II.[4] Then, as the decades passed, Soviet policy appeared to be intended to strengthen the status quo in Europe rather than overturn it. British policy-makers from the 1950s on did not believe that there was any likelihood of deliberate Soviet aggression against Western Europe. Nevertheless, in view of the concentration of military forces in Central Europe, the outbreak of war – as a result of crises during which policy-makers lost control of events – remained a contingency to guard against.

Soviet foreign policy in the Khrushchev era, during which the Soviet Union emerged as a strategic nuclear power, was plagued with contradictions. While maintaining an emphasis in its declared policy on detente and peaceful co-existence, and proclaiming that ideological competition with capitalism had shifted to the economic sphere, the Soviet leadership under Khrushchev quite overtly attempted to exploit strategic power for the attainment of foreign policy objectives. The clearest example was the Berlin crisis of 1958–62, when Khrushchev put pressure on the Western allies with a series of ultimatums whose apparent objective was to remove any Western presence from West Berlin. The crisis resolved itself after the building of the Berlin Wall. The culmination of missile diplomacy

Introduction

was the Cuban missile crisis of 1962. It must be remembered how palpably close to war the world seemed to be in Berlin and Cuba. The Soviet threat then seemed real enough, even if in retrospect we now interpret the dangers of those crises differently. The growing Soviet interest in the Third World, backed up by Soviet military power, intensified Western perceptions of the aggressiveness of Khrushchev's foreign policy.

The experiences of Berlin and Cuba induced a great sense of caution about the use of military power in the nuclear era. Despite the invasion of Czechoslovakia in 1968, the likelihood of war in Europe seemed to recede. Indeed, if Soviet policy towards Eastern Europe was designed to stabilize the status quo, the intervention in Czechoslovakia could be interpreted as enhancing the prospects for peaceful coexistence. In the era of detente and *Ostpolitik*, East and West began a process of normalizing relations on the basis of the territorial status quo and containing the military competition through arms control. The central dilemma remained that the Soviet Union was defining its security interests in ways incompatible with Western security requirements. Even though the West was now to a certain extent willing to accept Soviet influence in Eastern Europe, it sought to use the CSCE process to impose certain limits on it. The continued growth in Soviet strategic and theatre nuclear power, its involvement in conflicts in the Third World, the failure of conventional arms control and the refusal of the Soviet Union to fulfil the commitments of the Helsinki agreements all perpetuated the sense of a continuing East-West conflict. The period of the second Cold War in the early 1980s was characterized by a widespread sense of the dangers inherent in East-West confrontation.

It is not surprising that the advent of the new thinking under the Gorbachev leadership has focused attention particularly on East-West relations and their security dimension. If Gorbachev is serious about a new approach to international relations, about basing security on political rather than military instruments, then the prospect opens up of a new security system in Europe in which there is no longer a threat of large-scale military confrontation. The Cold War might truly come to an end. It is understandable, therefore, that much political attention has been paid to arms control and arms reduction regimes which promise to transform the military landscape in Europe.

Like the new political thinking in general, the substantial shifts in

Introduction

Soviet military doctrine and declared strategy and the new style in arms control are subject to a variety of different interpretations. At one end of the spectrum is the view that essentially nothing has changed.[5] As recently as 1988, William F. Scott and Harriet Fast Scott, two highly respected analysts of Soviet military literature, expressed it in the following terms:

> After Mikhail Gorbachev became the Communist Party's General Secretary, new slogans appeared in support of the image he sought to project. Although some of the words have been altered, the substance remains ... whoever may be the Party's General Secretary, it is improbable that any change will alter the Marxist-Leninist goal of scientific communism: the overthrow of capitalism, which in the final analysis means any nation outside of the Soviet orbit. This objective will remain the basic thrust of Soviet military doctrine.[6]

This is very similar to the view consistently expressed by former US Defence Secretary Caspar Weinberger. Among Western Sovietologists who support it are James Sherr and Gerhard Wettig. One gets the feeling, however, that in its most extreme formulation this view is tautologous in nature, because it is not susceptible to empirical refutation. Since virtually any foreign policy action by a state can be interpreted as being designed to strengthen the power of that state, and tactical retreats as well as advances are conceivable in the framework of the gradual achievement of the victory of world socialism, both overtly hostile political manoeuvres (e.g. an arms build-up) and conciliatory gestures (e.g. concessions in arms control) can be interpreted as fitting into a fundamentally offensive political strategy. The reaction of some Western defence experts to the INF agreement is instructive. Gorbachev's acceptance of large asymmetrical reductions in missile deployments was not interpreted by them as intended to reduce the confrontation with the West, but rather as the consequence of a more intelligent calculation of Soviet interests in that confrontation.[7] A variant of this view states that the Gorbachev leadership is genuinely interested in a period of relaxation of tension with the West because of the economic difficulties the Soviet Union faces. However, this is merely a temporary respite, after which the confrontation is to be resumed. Needless to say, all these interpretations stress the continuity between current and past

Soviet policy. They furthermore assume a large degree of consensus about the long-term goals of Soviet foreign policy within the Soviet decision-making system, even if there are disagreements about medium-range tactics.

The large majority of scholars and political leaders in the West, however, appear to have adopted the view that there is something genuinely new about Gorbachev's approach to security policy, even if they may not agree about the substance. The view expounded by Michael MccGwire is that since the mid-1960s Soviet military doctrine has been adapted to reduce the likelihood of nuclear war, and the new political thinking on security is the culmination of a trend that has lasted for twenty years.[8] Another view states that the Soviet Union is a power in decline, and that the new political thinking is simply an attempt to adapt to the new international environment in which the country finds itself. This view is based on the perception of a reduction in Soviet capabilities to sustain a particular role in the international system.[9] It may or may not mean that a fundamental and permanent shift in Soviet ideology and foreign policy is taking place. Others have argued that generational and sociological changes in the Soviet Union have enabled the new thinking to take hold.

The recent changes in Eastern Europe constitute perhaps the most eloquent refutation of the views held by such observers as Marie Mendras, Scott and Scott, and Weinberger. One can also point to a number of important studies which have explored the fundamental shifts in Soviet thinking that have occurred.[10] The present study proceeds on the assumption that the new thinking is not merely propaganda and that serious changes are indeed taking place in Soviet security policy. What are the implications for Soviet military policy? Are the changes in declared military doctrine matched by changes in Soviet force posture? What is the role of arms control in a transition to a more stable security regime in Europe? This book will give a general survey of recent Soviet military doctrine and capabilities, covering all aspects from strategic nuclear to conventional forces in order to give a picture of the impact of the new political thinking, such as it may be, on the totality of Soviet military power.

Chapter 2 will review the evolution of Soviet military doctrine, starting with the debate about the implications of nuclear weapons after the death of Stalin, and moving through the Khrushchev era, with its emphasis on nuclear missiles and strategic nuclear war, to

Introduction

the compromises of the early Brezhnev period and the recognition of mutual vulnerability in an age of strategic parity as codified in the SALT agreements and the shift to a strategy predicated on keeping any future conflict below the nuclear threshold. These developments form the background for the main issues to be discussed, namely the radical rethinking of Soviet military doctrine that appears to have begun under Gorbachev but clearly contains elements that predate his leadership. This chapter sets the scene for all the others, and individual themes addressed are elaborated in later chapters.

Chapter 3 will develop the general political context in which security policy is formulated. It will outline the political challenges facing the Gorbachev leadership, focusing in particular on the Soviet economy. It will briefly analyse the priorities on Gorbachev's political agenda of perestroika and draw out some of the implications for Soviet foreign policy. This chapter will also describe the institutional setting in which policy is formulated. A phenomenon of particular significance is the rise of the civilian arms control community in research institutes like IMEMO and ISKAN; these have provided the political leadership with an alternative source of expertise on arms control and disarmament issues, independent of the military. A principal issue in this chapter will be an assessment of the extent to which Gorbachev has been able to gain control of the decision-making. A particularly useful indicator will be personnel changes in the military, notably the changes in the top command, including the Ministry of Defence, and most recently the replacement of the Chief of the General Staff.

Chapter 4 is concerned with strategic nuclear forces. After a brief historical review of the evolution of Soviet strategic arms policy, this chapter will conduct a survey of the present Soviet strategic force posture. The main issues addressed will be the nature of the Soviet strategic threat, with particular emphasis on counterforce capabilities. Current trends with regard to the development of heavy ICBMs, mobile single-warhead missiles and new strategic bombers will be examined and future Soviet options analysed. The clarification of the rationales behind the Soviet force posture will provide the background for a discussion of arms control options. Particular emphasis will be placed on START and beyond. Soviet views about minimum nuclear deterrence postures as the goal of strategic arms reductions are also discussed.

Chapter 5 examines ballistic missile defence – a subject about which Soviet military literature has had relatively little to say since the ABM Treaty. The reasons which led the Soviet Union to sign the ABM Treaty are still subject to controversy in the West. This chapter will briefly set out the key features of the controversy about ballistic missile defence in the Soviet military and political establishment prior to the ABM Treaty, and identify the thinking that lay behind the abandonment of large-scale strategic defences. It will then seek to draw appropriate conclusions which permit an assessment of the Soviet response to SDI and possible future developments in the context of the general strategic environment. The place of strategic defence in arms control negotiations and its possible implications for British strategic force modernization will then be discussed.

Chapter 6 deals with theatre nuclear weapons. Soviet theatre nuclear capability has been at the centre of the (Western) security debate during the last ten years. The INF Treaty signed in 1987 eliminates long-range and medium-range theatre nuclear forces on both sides. This chapter constitutes a review of the evolution of Soviet theatre capabilities and assesses the significance of the INF Treaty.

Chapter 7 treats conventional forces. Soviet military doctrine has for most of the postwar period had a very strongly offensive orientation. Military reasons brought about a shift in Soviet military thought in the 1980s towards greater emphasis on defensive operations, and the need to re-evaluate the offensive/defensive mix in conventional strategy has been clearly recognized. At the same time, scholars in the policy institutes have criticized the offensive orientation of Soviet military doctrine. Calls for 'reasonable sufficiency', 'defensive defence' and a force posture which precludes the ability to overrun the opponent's territory have won the evident approval of the political leadership. This chapter will examine the meaning of these concepts as they are found in recent Soviet literature, and will seek to relate them to military writing about defensive military doctrine. It will seek to delineate areas of divergence between political writers (and their patrons in the political leadership) and military leaders about Soviet military doctrine, and what the implications are in terms of force posture and weapons procurements. Finally, some suggestions will be made about the possible outcomes of this debate and the consequences for Western security policy, particularly with regard to nuclear and conventional arms control.

Introduction

The last chapter will use the results of the analysis to assess the different prevailing interpretations of recent developments in Soviet security policy and to suggest likely future situations. It will review the general interests of the West and seek to identify options for the West in its security policies vis-à-vis the Soviet Union in the 1990s.

2
SOVIET MILITARY DOCTRINE

Soviet military policy is based on a highly developed body of thought known as military doctrine. As defined in an authoritative article in 1969, military doctrine represents the policy of the Communist Party and the Soviet government in the military arena:

> In considering the content of military doctrine we usually distinguish between its political and its military-technical principles. The political principles include the propositions revealing the socio-political essence of the war which the imperialists can unleash upon the Soviet Union, the character of the political objectives and the strategic tasks of the state in it and their influence on the construction of the armed forces and the methods of preparing for and waging war ... Military doctrine and strategy are a reflection of the general political objectives of the Soviet state and objectives in war – by this very process the CPSU leadership also determines the political principles of military doctrine.[1]

In the early post-Stalin period during the 1950s, the Soviet military still conceived of nuclear war as basically a more destructive version of World War II. The establishment of the Strategic Rocket Forces in December 1959 was accompanied by a revision in Soviet military doctrine. In a speech before the Supreme Soviet in January 1960, Khrushchev declared the primary importance of nuclear weapons and missiles. He emphasized that many of the traditional armed forces, such as air forces, surface navies and large standing armies, were becoming obsolete, that the initial phase of a nuclear war would probably be decisive and that such a war would be of short duration.

Military opposition to Khrushchev's 'one-sided' emphasis on nuclear weapons, the emerging strategic nuclear parity between the Soviet Union and the United States,[2] and the adoption of 'flexible response' by NATO led to a shift in Soviet military thought: the avoidance of escalation to a strategic nuclear level became a positive objective of Soviet military doctrine. Thus a shift occurred rather gradually in the period from the mid-1960s to the mid-1970s – away from the perception of global nuclear war as the most likely mode of a future conflict with the West, and towards planning for prolonged conflict below the nuclear threshold or on a theatre nuclear level. By the mid-1970s the General Staff Military Academy was teaching officers that in the event of a conflict in Western Europe it was expected that NATO, rather than the WTO, would initiate the use of nuclear weapons.[3] Alongside this new recognition of the significance of a conventional phase in a future war in Central Europe, there was a clear decision to achieve strategic nuclear parity with the United States. The third-generation ICBMs, which would form the backbone of Soviet strategic forces, were the SS-9 and the SS-11. The SS-9 was deployed at a constant rate of 49 missiles per year, levelling off at a total of about 280 missiles, whereas in the case of the SS-11 some 720 had been deployed by 1970.

Despite SALT I, both the United States and the Soviet Union substantially increased and modernized their strategic arsenals. This was possible mainly as a result of the development of MIRVs: SALT I limited missile launchers, not the number of warheads carried by each missile. The fourth-generation ICBM force, consisting primarily of the highly accurate SS-19 with six warheads (360 missiles deployed) and the heavy SS-18 (308 missiles, mostly deployed in an eight- to ten-warhead configuration), gave the Soviet Union a substantial counterforce capability (ability to strike military targets) in relation to the United States. The mid-1970s also saw the deployment of SLBMs of intercontinental range.

The public position of the Soviet leadership in the 1970s emphasized the reality of nuclear strategic parity and mutual assured destruction (MAD). As confidence grew that the United States could be deterred from engaging in a strategic nuclear attack on the Soviet Union (the corollary being that the Soviet Union was deterred from attacking the continental United States), Soviet policy shifted from that of nuclear pre-emption, which had appeared necessary in the 1950s in view of the threat of a surprise attack, to one of launch-on-warning. The 1970s saw the development and strengthening of theatre conventional and nuclear capabilities. The primary objective in a war in the European theatre would now be to deny NATO the option of mobilizing its resources and exercising its options for escalation. This could be done only by the rapid occupation of Western Europe and the elimination of American bases (the presence of which would make Great Britain a particular target), thus presenting the United States with the *fait accompli* of having been excluded from Europe. This strategy was of course greatly complicated by the presence of LRTNF and British and French nuclear forces.

The nuclear predicament: Soviet military policy in the early 1980s
The acceptance of nuclear parity and the abandonment of the pursuit of superiority were clearly set out in Brezhnev's well-known speech in Tula in January 1977. He went so far as to provide the rationale for a policy of not being the first to use nuclear weapons, and the same year the Warsaw Treaty Organization proposed a multilateral treaty on 'no first use'. A unilateral 'no first use' pledge was made in 1982.[4] However, the strategic and operational implications were not readily accepted by the Soviet military, and it is evident that the development of nuclear and conventional warfighting capabilities continued, along with naval deployments which helped to create the capability to project power on a global scale.

In the United States some prominent analysts interpreted Brezhnev's Tula speech as mere propaganda and drew public attention to the 'window of vulnerability' created by the alleged emerging Soviet capability to destroy the entire American ICBM force in a first strike. This ignored the technical difficulties and uncertainties associated with such a venture. It also ignored the substantial second-strike capability of the relatively invulnerable American SLBM force, as Chief of the General Staff Ogarkov pointed out. The Soviet Union must have been even more alarmed by the emerging US counterforce capability (both the MX and the Trident II are capable of destroying hard targets such as the ICBM sites in a high number of cases). While the United States had less than a quarter of its strategic warheads deployed on ICBMs, the figure for the Soviet Union was about 70 per cent. Furthermore, as David Holloway has pointed out: 'There is little evidence in Soviet thinking of the kind of technological hubris that would be required to launch such a horrendously risky strike.'[5]

None the less, Ogarkov, who was promoted to Chief of the General Staff in 1977 (almost one year after Dmitry Ustinov became Defence Minister), while paying lip-service to the official position, clearly advocated a nuclear war-fighting strategy and defended the 'objective possibility of achieving victory' in such a war. In 1981 Brezhnev reasserted the principle of mutual assured destruction, and went as far as denying the possibility of victory in nuclear war:

> ... it is dangerous madness to try to defeat each other in an arms race, to count on victory in nuclear war ... I will add that only he who has decided to commit suicide can start a nuclear war in the hope of emerging victorious from it. Whatever strength the attacker may have and whatever means of starting a nuclear war he may choose, he will not achieve his aims. Retaliation is unavoidable. That is our essential view.[6]

This statement came after the 26th Party Congress in March 1981 had decided a significant shift of resources away from defence and towards the civilian sector. A few months earlier Ogarkov had published an article in *Kommunist* which, while not directly contradicting the Brezhnev-Ustinov line and cleverly making use of Brezhnev's statements for his own purposes, none the less constituted a clear criticism of the official view. It defended a war-fighting strategy and advocated the maintenance of Soviet military power. This was reinforced in a pamphlet by Ogarkov published in 1982, in which he emphasized that both nuclear and conventional weapons would need to be integrated into operational planning.[7]

The military literature in 1982, at a time when Soviet theatre military capabilities were increasing, indicates a renewed emphasis on the role of nuclear weapons, despite the 'no first use' policy. The impending deployment of Pershing II and GLCMs in Europe were presumably an important factor. The debate was obviously also part of the internal battle for resources, since in October 1982 Brezhnev addressed military concerns about defence allocations directly, essentially telling an unusual meeting of several hundred high-ranking military officers that they would have to make the best of existing resource allocations. Ogarkov's remarks were sharply rebutted by Defence Minister Dmitry Ustinov, who reaffirmed the official party line, while tacitly acknowledging resistance from some quarters. Ustinov's very strong support for MAD and his harsh critique of Ogarkov's views failed to whip the military into line. The Soviet Union had fallen into a state of political paralysis, as Brezhnev's health deteriorated.

It is important to point out, however, that while Ogarkov apparently resisted certain aspects of the party line, he none the less supported the trend towards increasing conventional capabilities with the object of raising the nuclear threshold. Here we can discern a parallel to the debates within NATO, where 'war-fighting' strategists resisted the insight that the primary usefulness of nuclear weapons was not military but political. Substituting the role of battlefield nuclear weapons by conventional weapons based on new technologies (such as precision-guided munitions), which was part of NATO's Long-Term Defence Programme (LTDP) in the 1970s, was strongly advocated by Ogarkov in the early 1980s. The development of deep-strike strategies based on the Operational Manoeuvre Group (OMG) concept is another part of the Ogarkov 'revolution' in Soviet military affairs.[8] Ogarkov was also a vocal advocate of increased military spending and questioned the value of East-West detente and arms control agreements with the United States.

Andropov appeared to be determined to end the debates and impose party authority. He succeeded at least in damping down the controversy and eliciting formal agreement from Ogarkov. Meanwhile the party leadership itself was moving towards a far more pessimistic assessment of the international situation, resulting in increased military allocations (including the 'counter-deployments' after NATO's LRTNF deployment began).[9] Ogarkov was removed from his position in 1984, but remained a significant figure in the Soviet military. His successor, Marshal Sergei Akhromeev, held views similar to Ogarkov (except for a somewhat more positive view of possible improvements in East-West relations).

The pessimistic assessment of the world situation in 1983, the perception of an increased risk of war and the resentment against the Reagan administration resulted in a debate in the party leadership about the future of relations with the West. Eventually those favouring a more conciliatory line and a return to negotiations won through, as became evident by September 1984. Statements about military allocations at the time indicate a decision that while some additional resources would be made available, the general budgetary shift of 1981 would be implemented.[10]

Under the leadership of Brezhnev, Andropov and Chernenko, the Soviet Union attempted to restore detente and achieve arms control agreements more or less on the same terms and by the same tactics as before. While the breakdown in the consensus about nuclear defence policy in NATO countries as a result of the 'neutron bomb' and the controversies over INF had the effect of forcing NATO governments to give formal support to the process of negotiations, the old approach proved inadequate in the face of the more hostile international climate and the fervently anti-Soviet stance of the Reagan administration.

The need for a new departure was increasingly recognized by Soviet arms control experts. An important development was the acknowledgment that the arms race has an inherent dynamic of its own and that the Soviet Union has also contributed (or at least must be careful not to contribute) to it. Since the early days of strategic arms control, the journalist Alexander Bovin had stressed the need for the two sides not to threaten each other; in an article about INF in 1979 there was an explicit recognition that the West might also feel threatened by Soviet deployments.[11] Genrikh Trofimenko of ISKAN has also acknowledged the potential for 'mutual distrust'.[12] Aleksei Arbatov of IMEMO and Sergei Patrushev of IMRD stressed the 'self-perpetuating' character of the arms race, which undermines the picture of the Soviet Union making a controlled and rational response to Western attempts to achieve military superiority.[13] Oleg Bykov of IMEMO described the arms race as an action-reaction phenomenon, in which Soviet 'reactions' can be interpreted by the United States as 'actions' requiring further reactions, and admitted that Soviet 'countermeasures' may constitute a form of overinsurance.[14] The important implication for arms control policy was that it was no longer necessary to match every new American capability, and numerical equality was no longer as essential to a successful arms control regime. One of the issues which has had a particular impact on academic thinking has been the universality of the threat of nuclear destruction. Scientific modelling predicting the outbreak of 'nuclear winter' has found widespread acceptance among experts from the Academy of Sciences.

These ideas, which have had an increasing influence among the Soviet leadership, have been received with some scepticism by the military.[15] Nevertheless, the catastrophic nature of nuclear war, and hence the importance of avoiding such a war, have been accepted. In 1985, the Deputy Chief of the General Staff, M.A. Gareev, published a much-acclaimed book on Frunze which has been widely accepted as an official revision of the hitherto standard text edited by Sokolovsky, *Military Strategy*. With regard to the Sokolovsky volume, Gareev states that 'over more than 20 years not all the provisions of this book have been confirmed.'[16] In particular:

> In the 1960s and 1970s, the authors of this and many other books proceeded primarily from the view that a war, under all circumstances, would be waged employing nuclear weapons and military operations employing solely conventional weapons were viewed as a brief episode at the start of a war. However, the improvement and stockpiling of nuclear missile weapons have reached such limits where the massed employment of these weapons in a war can entail catastrophic consequences for both sides. At the same time in the armies of the NATO countries there has been a rapid process of modernizing conventional types of weapons. The main emphasis has been put on the development of highly accurate, guided weapons which in terms of effectiveness are close to low-power nuclear weapons. Under these conditions, as is assumed in the West, there will be greater opportunity for conducting a comparatively long war employing conventional weapons and primarily new types of high-precision weapons.[17]

This statement hints at the fact that, in the view of the Soviet military, the most important arena of military competition with the United States has become that of modern technologies for conventional warfare. Although the Soviet Union currently enjoys a quantitative advantage, Soviet military literature recognizes a shift towards the qualitative as the real basis for military power. Thus it is recognized that the 'emerging technology' of new conventional weapons has initiated a radical shift in military affairs.

Gareev identifies the central problem of military competition with the United States very clearly. Each new generation of weapons is much more sophisticated and considerably more expensive than the previous generation. It is therefore easily foreseeable that at some point the need to keep up in the arms race will exceed the economic and technological capabilities of one of the protagonists. Although the problems of the Soviet economy and the technology gap with the West are not addressed explicitly, Gareev nevertheless hints at how this appears from the perspective of the Soviet military:

> Here, it must be considered that the arms race caused by the imperialists is assuming an unprecedented scale, weapons are becoming ever more expensive and we are opposed by enemies that are economically significantly more powerful than ever before. For this reason, military-theoretical thought should be working constantly on how to most rationally utilize the means allocated for military needs within the limits of strict necessity so that defense be reliable and at the same time not too burdensome for the state.[18]

To summarize: at the political level, there was a reappraisal of the nature of the military competition with the West and of Soviet political interests. At the same time, the nature of the military competition was changing dramatically for military-technical reasons. The links between these disparate developments consisted, first, in the catastrophic nature of nuclear war, which made the avoidance of such conflict of paramount importance from both the political and the military-technical standpoints, and, second, in the economic difficulties of the Soviet Union, which made the military competition with the United States politically unsustainable and extremely problematic from a military-technical point of view.

New political thinking
The dramatic developments of the late 1980s represented a radical shift in the political aspect of military doctrine. Soon after Gorbachev came to power in 1985 his determination to engage the Soviet Union in a process of fundamental political and economic reform began to manifest itself. It was evident that this new political thinking, as it came to be called, required a different conceptual

framework. The resolution of the internal and external political problems facing the Soviet leadership required a degree of institutional and organizational change so far-reaching that nothing less than a fundamental reinterpretation of the meaning of Marxism-Leninism would do to legitimize it. In its foreign policy dimension it involved the assumption that a genuine and enduring relaxation of tension in East-West relations and a significant restraint in the arms competition were important prerequisites for the success of the policy of domestic perestroika. The driving force behind the new thinking is the perception that, in the long term, competition with the United States for military power is unsustainable on the basis of a weak economy. For Gorbachev, 'new political thinking' has become the ideological handle to manage the institutional change required by perestroika.

Previous arms control negotiations and arguments had been based on the concept of parity. This, however, had been interpreted in too rigid a manner. The only way in which the Soviet Union could extricate itself from the rigidity of its own and the American positions was by introducing a new set of concepts. The first of these was that of strategic stability, which had been central to Western arms control theory for quite some time, but which was now expanded and given new meaning in the Soviet debate. The concept of strategic stability was used to show that parity was not enough and that the constant pursuit of this goal could result in a situation of instability. One of the great weaknesses of official Western approaches to arms control has been the lack of any clear analysis of the ultimate direction and objectives of substantial arms reductions such as were envisaged in the START process. A new guiding principle has been introduced into the Soviet discourse on force posture and arms control. It is called 'reasonable sufficiency'.

The first reference to this principle came during Gorbachev's visit to France in 1985. In February 1986, at the 27th Party Congress, Gorbachev used the phrase 'reasonable adequacy' to refer to the need to lower the levels of all types of military capabilities. Since this time the concept has developed substantially, and use of the term (or a rough equivalent) has become commonplace among political leaders, academics and intellectuals, and the military. The precise meaning of 'reasonable sufficiency' is not clear, and the expression is subject to considerable debate in the Soviet Union. What is clear, though, is that it is primarily a political concept, designed to replace the language of arms control and a continuing arms race.[19] Civilian experts have argued that the arms race represents a common threat to mankind, and that a more flexible approach to the concept of 'strategic parity' should be adopted. They have stressed the value of 'unilateral measures'. In particular, the principle of 'sufficiency' implies the possibility of asymmetric force reductions.

Reasonable sufficiency in its political dimension symbolizes the non-aggressive objectives of Soviet military policy. Conflict in international relations is to be resolved through political means. In its military dimension, sufficiency implies abandoning the notion that superiority is a necessary and sufficient condition for victory. The military potential of the Soviet Union must be sufficient to be able to rebuff any form of external aggression, but must not be seen to pose a threat to other states.[20] The influence of this way of thinking has been evident in Soviet arms control policy under Gorbachev. He has shown a far greater degree of flexibility than before, proposing initiatives and making unilateral gestures which have often surprised the West, as well as accepting far greater openness to verification. In short, the policies appear to be leading towards a substantial demilitarization. This is indicated by the announcement of the goal of eliminating all nuclear weapons by the year 2000, the signing of the INF Treaty (which eliminated an entire class of nuclear weapons) and the objective of mutual reductions in conventional force levels to one of 'reasonable sufficiency'.

Another component in this trend has been the introduction of the notion of a 'defensive defence' – a force posture which is purely defensive in character. There is a wide spectrum of views about the precise meaning of a defensive military doctrine. Opinion ranges from the view of some military leaders that Soviet military doctrine always has been defensive and thus no changes in force posture are required, to the view that in the case of large-scale enemy attack a counteroffensive may be necessary but that it should stop at the boundary of the enemy's territory, and the view that any idea of a counteroffensive should be abandoned and a force posture should be developed which provides an adequate defence but does not involve offensive capabilities.[21] Although these debates have not been resolved, the defensive character of Soviet military doctrine and the principle of 'sufficiency' have now been enshrined in the official statement of Soviet military doctrine.

The new political thinking has resulted in a redefinition of the

Soviet military doctrine

entire concept of military doctrine. In the words of Akhromeev, 'Soviet military doctrine is a system of fundamental views on the essence *and prevention of* war'.[22] [Emphasis added] Similarly, Deputy Chief of Staff M. A. Gareev declared in 1988 that war prevention had become the principal goal of Soviet military doctrine.[23] Thus, by the late 1980s, it had become clear from a variety of official statements that the following now constituted the fundamental principles of Soviet military doctrine:

(1) The prevention of war is the most fundamental objective of Soviet military doctrine.
(2) No war can be considered to be the continuation of politics.
(3) Security is mutual.
(4) The primary means of enhancing security are political, not military-technical.
(5) Not only the political means of security but also the military-technical means should be 'defensive' in character.
(6) Soviet armed forces should be developed on the basis of the principle of 'reasonable sufficiency'.

The new Soviet thinking about what is required for the prevention of war is very different from the Western focus on deterrence. It recognizes the destabilizing nature of forces which appear to threaten the security interests of other nations, and thus calls for a defensive force posture on the basis of 'reasonable sufficiency'. In principle the Soviet force posture could be restructured along these lines on a unilateral basis, but most of the theoretical discussion, as well as the practical policy, has made it dependent on arms control negotiations with the purpose of developing an international security system based on the principle of sufficiency and non-threatening force postures.

One important issue is the role of nuclear weapons in current Soviet military doctrine. There has definitely been a convergence between Western and Soviet thinking on the deterrent function of nuclear weapons.[24] Nevertheless, Gorbachev seems to share the view of some Soviet civilian analysts that nuclear deterrence is unstable in the long term. The official position of the Soviet Union is still that the ultimate objective of nuclear arms reductions should be complete and global denuclearization. It is known, however, that the majority of Soviet arms control experts would prefer a negotiated transition to a stable minimum deterrent posture. This would be 'reasonable sufficiency' at the strategic nuclear level.

Conclusion
It is undeniable that Soviet military doctrine has undergone radical revision in recent years. The key issues on which Western interpretations diverge are the consequences of these changes for Soviet military and foreign policy objectives, and the resulting assessment of the Soviet Union as a military threat to the West. The most optimistic interpretation would be that the current Soviet leadership is genuinely determined to end the East-West confrontation and therefore seeks to initiate a process of demilitarizing East-West relations in the long term. A more cynical interpretation is that the Soviet Union is merely seeking a *peredyshka* (breathing-space) to solve its economic problems, with the implication that the East-West confrontation will be resumed at some point in the future. Yet another common interpretation is that the changes in military policy are designed merely to cut the 'dead wood' in the Soviet military and make it 'leaner and fitter': i.e. to use arms reductions in a process of military restructuring that will result in more efficient and modern armed forces. A fourth interpretation states that although there is a shift in the expression of military doctrine, this is merely a propaganda exercise: in terms of capabilities, force deployments and actual objectives, Soviet military policy has remained the same.

Although the Soviet economy does require a respite from military competition with the West, there is no evidence that the notion of a *temporary* shift in foreign and defence policy forms any part of military or political thinking. Nevertheless, some ambiguities do remain. This is because Soviet military doctrine derives from rather disparate sources, such as the development of military science by the military experts, on the one hand, and the radical departures of new political thinking by the political leadership on the other. Whereas the military input relates primarily to the adaptation of military thought to contemporary conditions – in other words, it concerns itself with the changes in the military-technical requirements to achieve its general objectives – the political leadership has introduced a completely new framework in which these objectives are to be defined. Since much of the military input is still based on old assumptions, there are inevitable tensions. In the controversies between civilian and military representatives over the future of the Soviet armed forces, Soviet military doctrine has become an instrument for both sides to make their views known. The ambiguities inherent in the conceptual framework of current Soviet military thinking are partly due to the practical difficulties in giving concepts like 'defensive defence' and 'reasonable sufficiency' a specific content, but they are also a reflection of a compromise between the political objectives of the leadership and the concerns of the professional military. Nevertheless, the scale and nature of the unilateral force reductions announced by Mikhail Gorbachev during his speech at the United Nations General Assembly against evident resistance from the military convinced many sceptics that the Soviet stated intentions of moving towards a less offensive force posture had to be taken seriously.

There are still fundamental differences of view between the Soviet civilian leadership and the military, and between the military aspects of Soviet new political thinking and Western conceptions of security requirements. Perhaps the most obvious relates to the continued need for nuclear deterrence. The important task in the realm of military thinking East and West is to establish the extent to which mutually acceptable conceptions of security requirements and policies can be developed to ensure a stable transition to a regime where the military confrontation ceases to be the defining characteristic of East-West relations.

3
THE SOURCES OF SOVIET SECURITY POLICY

The domestic sources of new political thinking
Western political scientists have a common tendency to explain the Soviet Union's behaviour in terms of its relations with the West. Thus Soviet military policy is often interpreted as part of a general strategy to achieve global domination, and similarly the impulse for the new thinking is judged to be the need to adapt to an environment where the Soviet Union is no longer capable of playing a global role and must therefore reduce its international aspirations. If, however, one looks carefully at the domestic context of Soviet foreign policy in the post-Stalin era, one can make a very good case for the primacy of domestic policy priorities. This is not to say that the Soviet Union's interaction with other powers is unimportant; rather, it is to affirm that its relations have to a great extent been designed on the basis of their effect on the domestic political environment.[1]

Similarly, it can be argued that the new political thinking is primarily a response to the systemic domestic crisis of the Soviet Union.[2] The primary focus of Western analysis is usually the economic situation, and there is no doubt that the Soviet economy has faced a decline of crisis proportions.[3] The steady decline in growth rates since the 1950s, the consistent underfulfilment of production targets, under-mechanization and the labour shortage, the extraordinary degree of waste in the centrally planned economy, the lack of infrastructure and the poor performance of agriculture are all part of the dismal story. More important even than the economic, however, have been the sociological factors. The increasing alienation from the regime of all strata of the population, but in particular the middle class and intelligentsia, which find themselves stifled and deprived of economic and non-material rewards, is the dominant feature of a social and political system 'in an advanced state of political breakdown',[4] as Seweryn Bialer puts it. The reassertion of nationalism in various parts of the Soviet Union, presenting it, as some observers have commented, with some fifteen potential 'Ulster-type scenarios' on its territory, is merely the most visible manifestation of the process of political and social disintegration. In private conversations with leading academics there is evidence of panic that unless the programme of perestroika succeeds, the Soviet Union will face a complete catastrophe.

Gorbachev's programme of economic and political reform will ultimately not be able to progress unless he can persuade the military to cooperate. Indeed, it is vital for him to gain control over the defence agenda, because military policy plays a key part in his endeavours to create a new international climate and to restructure the economy at home. The military is a powerful institution in Soviet society. It is responsible for the security of the Soviet Union and thus has an unrivalled source of expertise that gives its leadership substantial influence in shaping Soviet security policy. The defence industry consumes a large share of material and human resources; it gets the best materials, machinery and skilled workers. In the long term the economic future of the Soviet Union will depend on redirecting a large part of the resources that currently go into the military effort.

The dilemma that Gorbachev faces vis-à-vis the military has been with the Soviet Union for some considerable time. Khrushchev's relations with the military, for example, were dominated by this issue. The primary reliance on nuclear weapons, the cuts in conventional forces, the contradictory foreign policy (seeking detente and peaceful coexistence while at the same time engaging in risky adventures for the sake of foreign policy successes to placate his opponents) were all bound up with Khrushchev's domestic priorities: the restructuring of Soviet industry away from the heavy metal industries, relieving the shortage of manpower in the economy by reducing military manpower, and reallocating resources to consumer goods production and agriculture. In the post-Khrushchev era, the military regained greater control over the formulation of military doctrine and saw many of their budget demands satisfied, until in the late 1970s the deteriorating economic situation forced the Brezhnev leadership to put a brake on military spending, resulting in very strained party-military relations. Gorbachev faces similar, albeit even more acute, dilemmas. Before looking at the extent to which Gorbachev has been able to control the defence agenda, we need to examine some of the institutional mechanisms.

Soviet decision-making on defence

(i) The Politburo
Policy formulation in the Soviet Union is dominated by the Communist Party and in particular by its leadership in the Politburo. The Politburo (called the Presidium from 1953 to 1966) is formally elected by the Central Committee, but the real power relationships are reversed, since the Central Committee is largely appointed by the Politburo. The government, headed by the Premier and the Council of Ministers, plays the subordinate role of policy implementation, although in the early years of the post-Stalin era the relationship between party leadership and government was by no means constant. Malenkov was leader of the Soviet Union from the position of Premier. Khrushchev was both First Secretary and Premier for most of his time as Soviet leader. After his fall, his successors restored the principle of collective leadership. While, at first, state administrators had equal representation with political leaders in the Politburo, the party gradually began to assert greater control over the government as Brezhnev became more powerful, and instead of career specialists more and more party generalists tended to be appointed to the Council of Ministers.[5]

The Politburo is thus the central decision-making agency for all areas of national importance. It is therefore ultimately in control of defence policy; it determines the main lines of policy, it takes the major resource allocation decisions, approves budgets and is the final arbiter of any controversies that may arise. At times it has become involved directly with the development and procurement decisions on particular weapons systems. Its role in defence and foreign affairs was strengthened even more in 1973, when the ministers of these departments as well as the head of the KGB were made full members. During the Strategic Arms Limitation Talks in 1974, special sessions of the Politburo were convened to consider certain proposals.

It is evident, therefore, that the degree to which Gorbachev can determine Soviet military policy is governed by his ability to obtain Politburo approval for his policies. This is facilitated by the fact that the military currently has no voting representative in the Politburo. It is no coincidence that as Gorbachev has increased his power in the Politburo over the years by removing significant opponents (e.g. Romanov, Shcherbitsky) and reducing the influence of others (Ligachev), the military has been forced to take more notice of the new agenda in security policy.

(ii) The Defence Council

The Defence Council (*Sovet Oborony*) has been described as 'essentially a subcommittee of the Politburo'; this may be true in practice, but according to the 1977 Constitution it is a state and not a party institution.[6] It was established in the mid-1960s as an institution for the party leadership to control Soviet military policy. Its composition is determined by the Presidium of the Supreme Soviet. The General Secretary (as Chairman of the Defence Council), the Chairman of the Council of Ministers, the Minister of Defence, the Chairman of the KGB, the Minister for Foreign Affairs, the Secretary of the CPSU for Ideology and the Secretary of the CPSU Central Committee for Cadres are ex officio members. The Chief of the General Staff acts as the secretary of the Defence Council. The Defence Council concerns itself with military policy in the broadest sense, including questions of internal and external policy in economics, ideology and diplomacy. It also deals with decisions regarding the defence industries, important weapons developments and procurement, budgetary questions and manpower levels. It provides the guidelines at the start of the planning process and prepares recommendations to the Politburo once the plans have been finalized by the defence industries and the Ministry of Defence. These are then incorporated into the 'Military Development Plan' (*Plan voennogo stroitel'stva, podgotovki strany i vooruzhennykh sil k voine*).

Some light was thrown on the function of the Defence Council when it became apparent during the SALT I negotiations that it was the chief instrument whereby the political leadership involved itself in the process. It appears that the Defence Council resolved the final policy decisions with regard to SALT on behalf of the Politburo. At a time of radical change in Soviet military policy, the Defence Council is one of the major channels through which Gorbachev can exert control over the process. At the same time, it is dependent to a large extent on information input from the Ministry of Defence and the General Staff and is therefore also a forum in which the professional military can make its influence felt.[7]

(iii) The Ministry of Defence

The Ministry of Defence is the primary government agency responsible for the implementation of CPSU military policy. Structurally, there are three different loci of decision-making in the ministry: the centralized activities of the ministry itself, the General Staff and the five branches of the armed services. Although technically the ministry is a government agency, it stands apart from other ministries by virtue of its domination by the military. It thus represents a different constituency, which may be argued to form an interest group of its own.[8] The General Staff has been described as the 'brain of the army', responsible both for the formulation of military doctrine and for the coordination of its practical application:

> The General Staff comprehensively analyses and evaluates the developing military-political situation, determines the trends in the development of the means of waging war and the methods of their application, organizes the training of Armed Forces and ensures their high combat-readiness to repel any aggression.[9]

It is evident that the General Staff has been influential in important decisions on military policy. In the 1960s, for example, the then Chief of the General Staff, Matvei Zakharov, exercised crucial influence in support of the sustained build-up of the Soviet ICBM force and the decline of Soviet interest in ballistic missile defence.[10] Nikolai Ogarkov was engaged in a prolonged political struggle with the party leadership over defence allocations and nuclear strategy. The General Staff has had an important role in arms control negotiations, as witnessed by the presence of Ogarkov and Alekseev on Soviet delegations. It also has a Legal and Treaty Department;[11]

Chief of the General Staff S. Akhromeev was a prominent actor at the Reykjavik summit in 1986. But, as will be discussed in more detail later, the political leadership has other sources of expertise on arms control matters, and Akhromeev's resistance to the unilateral arms reductions announced in 1988 led to his resignation and a decline in the influence of the General Staff.

Some attention should also be drawn to the role of the Main Political Administration of the Soviet army and navy. It has a dual status as a department of the Central Committee Secretariat and as a directorate of the Ministry of Defence. It is responsible for party political work in the armed forces and has often played a key role in party-military relations. Its role under Gorbachev will be discussed later.

(iv) The conduct of foreign policy

Needless to say, the Ministry of Foreign Affairs plays a critical role in the implementation of security policy. It has direct responsibility for all relations with foreign countries and is also deeply involved in arms control matters. For this purpose it has its own arms control and disarmament section. The military office of the Minister for Foreign Affairs prepares reports on the world situation for the Defence Council. The removal of the veteran Foreign Minister A. A. Gromyko and his replacement by Eduard Shevardnadze on 2 July 1985 was an essential precondition for Gorbachev to establish his influence in foreign affairs. Since then, there has been a great deal of change in ministry personnel.

Another institution involved in the making of foreign policy is the Secretariat of the Central Committee with its various departments and commissions. One key Gorbachev adviser, A. N. Yakovlev, an active promoter of the new thinking, became chief of the Propaganda Department in 1985 and is now Chairman of the Central Committee Commission on International Policy. The realigned foreign policy establishment has been a useful instrument for Gorbachev in furthering innovations in security policy.

(v) The research institutes

The present network of foreign policy institutes was established as a result of a decision taken at the 20th Congress of the CPSU, after the Soviet leadership had become aware of the lack of expert analysis to shape foreign policy. The institutes had a political role from the start. Initially, they generally promulgated the Khrushchev line of peaceful coexistence. During the Brezhnev era, however, the political leadership sought clear advice from the academic community, with greater emphasis being placed on objectivity; IMEMO, the first institute to be established, became an important reservoir of expertise for the Central Committee. During the SALT period, a community of arms control experts formed in the academic institutions; Georgy Arbatov, the director of ISKAN, became a prominent adviser to Brezhnev. The members of this community of experts were of course very much part of the party elite, but, working in a somewhat independent academic environment, they found it possible to develop broader and more innovative approaches to Soviet security issues. The political role of the institutes consisted in projecting an image of the Soviet Union as a superpower equal with the United States and defending the policy of the Soviet leadership on detente and arms control.[12]

The foreign policy institutes, in particular IMEMO, ISKAN and the newly established Institute of Europe, have now become the intellectual power-houses of the new thinking. As has been pointed out, many elements of the new thinking had appeared in the academic literature already prior to the advent of the Gorbachev leadership; but there is no doubt that the political role of the institutes has been greatly enhanced. Prominent academics act as spokesmen for the leadership, interact with officials on committees and have close links with the top echelons of the Communist Party and Soviet government. Aleksandr Yakovlev, former director of IMEMO, has now risen to be the number two in the Politburo. Other new thinkers such as Vladimir Petrovsky, Evgeny Primakov and Georgy Shakhnazarov are in pivotal positions. In 1987 the Ministry of Foreign Affairs set up a small unit called the Scientific Centre which plays a coordinating role between the ministry and the research institutes of the Academy of Sciences, commissioning research, evaluating research proposals and passing on research reports to the appropriate directorates of the ministry. This constitutes one of the direct links between the Ministry of Foreign Affairs and the institutes, which give researchers a practical role in the process of policy formulation. A paradoxical feature of glasnost and the rise in the influence of the research institutes is that articles in academic journals no longer reflect official policy to the extent they did before; the margin of freedom to publish has widened considerably. Thus many of the radical ideas produced by the institutes are part of an ongoing and vigorous debate. As we shall see in the following chapters, however, there are many other cases when ideas proposed by leading academic advocates of the new thinking have been at least partially incorporated into policy. The foreign policy research institutes, therefore, have played a crucial role in providing expertise for the formulation of policy that originates from outside the established bureaucracy, and have contributed to the transformation of the intellectual framework in which Soviet security policy is conducted.[13]

(vi) The administration of the defence industries
The Council of Ministers is responsible for the industrial aspects of the 'military-industrial complex'. The Military-Industrial Commission (VPK, *Voenno-promyshlennaya kommissiya*) is an agency of the Council of Ministers responsible for coordinating the various organizations in the military, the party and the government involved with the procurement and production of weapons. Its chairman was Yury D. Maslyukov until he was promoted to Chairman of the State Planning Committee (Gosplan) on 6 February 1988; he was then replaced by I. S. Belousov. The defence industries submit their proposals to the VPK, where they are studied for their technical feasibility, production requirements and impact on other sectors of the economy. The VPK also studies funding arrangements, production methods and timetables. Some research institutes of the Academy of Sciences are apparently under VPK control; the VPK is involved with all aspects of military R&D throughout the Soviet Union and to some extent in the Warsaw Pact countries. If the VPK drafts a document on a weapons development proposal, this represents a decision binding on all parties once it has been approved by the Council of Ministers.

The Soviet defence industry is controlled by nine ministries subordinate to the Council of Ministers through the VPK and supervised also by the Defence Production Department of the CC Secretariat. In contrast to civilian industry, which has great difficulty in meeting its targets, the defence industry has a very generous allocation of resources and surplus capacity, which is used for civilian purposes when not otherwise needed. Under Gorbachev some organizational changes have been made which are designed to improve the management of technological progress and the integration of civilian and military production. According to Larrabee, these include: a new Machine-Building Bureau of the Council of Ministers established in October 1985 and headed by I. S. Silaev; a new State Committee for Computer Technology and Information Services headed by N. V. Gorshkov; a new department in the Academy of Sciences to improve the integration of research in areas with military application; and, finally, multi-branch scientific-technical complexes whose purpose is to integrate efforts throughout the R&D cycle.[14] The appointment of former defence industrialists to high-level positions in the civilian economy (e.g. Maslyukov and Silaev) is interpreted by Larrabee as part of a process whereby Gorbachev seeks to harness the resources of the defence industries to the civilian economy. Important here will be the conversion of defence industrial capacity to civilian use.

Party-military relations under Gorbachev
The unexpected absence of military representatives from the Lenin Mausoleum at Chernenko's funeral in March 1985 was an indication that the new leadership was emphasizing civilian control over the military from the start. As Chairman of the Defence Council (officially confirmed on 2 August 1985), Gorbachev moved relatively swiftly to develop mechanisms for taking responsibility in military affairs. He was helped by the shifts in the Politburo (notably the resignation of Romanov) as Politburo members also comprise much of the Defence Council. The next step was a shake-up of the Main Political Administration. Aleksei Epishev, chief of the MPA since the 1960s, was retired in July 1985 and replaced by Aleksei Lizichev, head of the Political Administration of the Group of Soviet Forces in Germany. The MPA became the main channel for the development of perestroika in the armed forces, starting with what Malcolm Mackintosh has described as 'a major shake-up of the political administrations of almost all of the main headquarters and commands of the Armed Forces'.[15]

Some of the old instruments of party control in the armed forces have been revived by the Gorbachev leadership. Thus there has been a renewed emphasis on party work and political and ideological education. Gorbachev has also stressed the old principle of *kritika/ samokritika* (criticism/self-criticism) which had been subject to attack from the professional military in the Khrushchev period.

Debate has even been started again about the principle of *edinonachalie* (one-man command). The content, however, is quite new. Perestroika in the armed forces is based on the same principles as in the economic sphere, the intention being to create an effective army, deal with laziness, inefficiency, lack of personal control, alcoholism, bullying (*dedovshchina*), friction between nationalities and educational backwardness, and emphasize personal responsibility and competence. It also aims to introduce the principles of glasnost and *demokratizatsiya* into the armed force. Although parts of this programme are welcomed by the military leadership, in that they are designed to remedy serious deficiencies in the armed forces, other aspects are less well received. Both glasnost and *demokratizatsiya* are somewhat contrary to the military spirit. During the Khrushchev era, the expression *edinonachalie na partiinoi osnove* ('one-man command on a party basis') was used to denote the interference of party officials in commanders' decisions. The professional military succeeded in having this practice banned and one-man command re-established. Now, the old formula of 'one-man command on a party basis' is being revived within the context of *demokratizatsiya*, implying that junior officers should have their say in the decision-making process and be able to exercise their initiative in implementing decisions reached by democratic means. The literature shows that the precise implications of this are not clear, and so the debate continues.[16]

The endeavour to strengthen political control over the armed forces was associated with significant changes in the High Command. The Commander-in-Chief of the Strategic Rocket Forces Vladimir Tolubko, who was 71, was replaced by Army General Yury Maksimov. The next major retirement was that of Admiral Gorshkov in December 1985, followed in 1986 by the retirement of the First Deputy Minister of Defence Vassily Petrov, the Commander of the Civil Defence Aleksandr Altunin, and the Army General in charge of Personnel Ivan Shkadov. Shkadov was replaced by the relatively unknown Dmitry Yazov. Yazov launched a programme of personnel changes designed to promote perestroika within the armed forces along the lines envisaged by the political leadership.[17] This was obviously necessary because, as a stream of statements from the political and MPA leadership indicate, in the second half of 1986 the process of perestroika in the armed forces was not making nearly enough progress. In a speech at the January 1987 Plenum

Gorbachev tackled this problem head on and quite explicitly threatened those who did not come up to the mark with dismissal.[18] As Dale Herspring has pointed out,

> In response to these unequivocal signals from Gorbachev, other top Soviet generals began to clamber onto the *perestroika* bandwagon. Numerous articles on the subject written by the Soviet military leadership appeared in the Soviet press early in 1987 ... those who did not support it wholeheartedly were severely criticized.[19]

A major opportunity to revamp the top military leadership came as a result of West German civilian Mathias Rust's landing of a Cessna on Red Square in May 1987. Among the casualties were Defence Minister Sergei Sokolov and the Commander-in-Chief of the Air Defence Forces Koldunov. The choice of Yazov to succeed Sokolov, although unexpected, appears logical in retrospect. Yazov's expertise was not in military thought, but rather in personnel and administration. He was therefore ideally suited to advance the Gorbachev programme of the reorganization of the armed forces.

To sum up, party-military relations under Gorbachev have been conducted according to the following objectives and principles:

(a) Rejuvenation of the High Command to facilitate the promotion of perestroika and the new thinking as well as improving cooperation of the military with the Gorbachev programme. As we shall see later, only recently has the military come, at least in its public statements, more fully behind the new thinking in military affairs.

(b) The pursuit of perestroika in the armed forces, including democratization and openness (the most visible signs of the latter being the publication of data on Soviet military deployments, including the hitherto classified Soviet designations of missile types, and the publication of an 'honest defence budget').

(c) The reduction of the military role in security policy decision-making. Significantly, the Minister of Defence is still only a Candidate Member of the Politburo. More importantly, there is a greater reservoir of civilian expertise on military affairs than before, principally due to the rise of the academic institutes. The at least partial loss by the General Staff of its monopoly on military information, aided by the encroachment of glasnost into the military sphere, widens the political leadership's options in decision-making. The outcome of the conflict over the unilateral arms reductions announced in Gorbachev's speech to the United Nations General Assembly in December 1988 was the resignation of Chief of the General Staff Akhromeev. His replacement by a relatively unknown outsider, General Moiseev, who had no particular expertise in military science, signalled a substantial diminution of the role of the General Staff in the decision-making institutions, particularly in the Defence Council, where Moiseev and Yazov are the only military representatives.

Controlling the military-industrial complex

Apart from the decision-making process of the Defence Council, the most effective method of civilian control over the military resides in the control over the defence budget exercised by the Defence and Security Committee of the Supreme Soviet. This control is rather limited at present owing to lack of glasnost about military expenditure. Although more realistic figures for the defence budget (77.3 billion roubles) and the outer space budget (6.9 billion roubles) have been published, the official defence budget still has to be treated with caution, given that in the Soviet military industry, as in the rest of the economy, prices bear no relation to cost.[20] Furthermore, there is no information on individual military programmes or on their cost. Any reduction in the military budget decreed by the Supreme Soviet is therefore across the board. This considerably inhibits parliamentary control.

The next step is obviously the conversion of military-industrial capacity to civilian purposes. Gorbachev himself has clearly committed himself to switch defence industries to the production of consumer goods.[21] In fact, many Soviet defence factories are already engaged in civilian production. A missile plant in Krasnoyarsk, for example, manufactures refrigerators; another missile factory at Dnepropetrovsk produces small tractors. In the spring of 1988 decisive steps were taken to engage the defence industries to a greater extent in production for the civilian economy. Some tank factories produce diesel engines and rail equipment; a reduction in tank production and increased output of civilian goods is thus a real option. Bicycles, motorcycles, televisions, radios and record-players are among the items produced by the defence industries. Within the VPK, a new directorate for civilian production has been created. Julian Cooper has reported on the new initiative:

> ... the radio industry (responsible for radar and computer systems) will make refrigeration equipment for the food industry and retail sector, the aviation and ground forces equipment industries will manufacture textile machinery, products of the shipbuilding industry will include equipment for restaurants and cafés, and the nuclear-weapons-producing Ministry of Medium Machine-building now has responsibility for making equipment for the dairy industry, including milking machines.[22]

This rapid expansion of civilian production by the defence industries is part of a substantial effort to shift resources from the military to the civilian sector, introducing greater economic accountability in the process. The policy was given increased momentum by the decision in December 1988 to reduce the Soviet armed forces by 12% (500,000 men), the military budget by 14.2% and arms production by 19.5%.[23] Measures taken included the establishment of a special permanent service by the Soviet air force to transport civilian cargo – 45,000 tonnes in 1989. Military equipment and supplies that can be used for civilian purposes such as fuel, cars, small ships and radio equipment worth a total of 500 million roubles are to be put up for sale.[24] One of the most visible symbols of the effort to use military assets for civilian purposes was the conversion of trucks designed to transport SS-20 missiles dismantled under the INF Treaty: they will be used for hoisting cranes. The conversion of the military industries, however, has met with fundamental problems which have been elaborated in some detail by Aleksei Izyumov:

(a) There was no general plan for conversion. Military enterprises were suddenly informed about decisions to cancel or curtail military production after the December 1988 decision. They had substantial difficulties in redesigning production processes and finding new suppliers and customers. Some adopted a 'wait and see' attitude and have resisted conversion to civilian production.

(b) In the conversion of military industry often little attention is paid to the technological profile of the factories concerned, thus making the process difficult and wasting existing equipment.

(c) There is no clear strategy about the scope and limits of conversion, or about the shape of the military-industrial capacity the Soviet Union would seek to retain. This particular problem is compounded by the lack of military glasnost.

Despite these difficulties, it is evident that the Gorbachev leadership has made great efforts in controlling and redirecting the resources allocated to the defence industries.

In January 1989 a new National Commission was formed under the chairmanship of Academician Vsevolod Avdnevsky to study the problems of conversion. It involves representatives from the VPK, Gosplan, the Ministry of Finance and the Soviet Peace Committee, together with a variety of public figures including Abel Aganbegyan and Marshal Kulikov. It has four committees to study the economic aspects, the social aspects (this involves the trade unions in particular), the scientific and technological aspects and the international aspects of conversion. It has no formal role in the governmental decision-making process, but rather serves as an educational and political lobby. It sees as one of its principal tasks to work out the agenda for a large conference to be held in Moscow in June 1990 under United Nations auspices.

The net result is that Gorbachev has made substantial progress in the past four years in taking control over the defence agenda. Soviet military doctrine has been reshaped to conform with the new thinking, and significant progress has been made in arms control. We also see the beginnings of a restructuring of the Soviet armed forces (see Chapter 7) and substantial arms reductions and military spending cuts. In conjunction with this, as already noted, much emphasis is now being placed on the conversion of defence industrial capacity to civilian uses. The extent to which Gorbachev will be able to continue will depend in part on the evolution of the international security environment, particularly on the rapid changes in Eastern Europe, as well as on the success of economic and political reform at home.

4
STRATEGIC ARMS POLICY

The Soviet Union and strategic arms
When Stalin died in 1953, the Soviet Union had a limited stockpile of atomic bombs and only what by American standards were obsolescent bombers to deliver them (the range of the TU-4 was insufficient for two-way missions to the continental United States). It was not until 1954 that nuclear weapons began to be integrated into the Soviet armed forces and their training. However, Stalin had initiated a comprehensive research-and-development programme to produce nuclear weapons and improve delivery vehicles, and this continued to progress. In August 1953 the USSR exploded a thermonuclear device. Among other new developments were a twin-turbojet medium-range bomber (the Badger) and two modern types of heavy bomber with intercontinental range (the four-jet Bison and the multi-turboprop Bison).

These developments led to fears in the United States that the Soviet Union might be on the brink of a mass production programme of long-range bombers which might result in a 'bomber gap'. The gap, however, did not materialize. In 1955 the Soviet Union still possessed no delivery systems of intercontinental range, while the United States had 1,309 bombers which could deliver 2,310 warheads (plus 698 warheads deployed on forward bases). The Soviet Union could deliver a total of 324 warheads on systems with regional range. Instead of competing with the United States in the deployment of strategic bombers, Khrushchev sought rapidly to change the perception of the strategic balance by moving the Soviet Union into the missile age. American fears of the emerging strategic nuclear capabilities of the Soviet Union were dramatically heightened by the Soviet launch in October 1957 of the first earth satellite, Sputnik. This demonstrated to the world that the Soviet Union possessed the technology to develop intercontinental ballistic missiles.

However, these fears turned out to be unwarranted. The first-generation ICBM (the SS-6) was never deployed in more than token numbers. It was plagued with technical difficulties that made it unsuitable as a delivery vehicle for nuclear weapons: it used a highly unstable propellant which could not be stored, making launching difficult, and furthermore it needed ground stations for guidance. Its guidance system was also subject to disruption by electronic interference. By 1960 the Soviet Union had deployed a total of four ICBMs and 145 strategic bombers.[1]

Second- and third-generation missiles with intercontinental range, the SS-7, SS-8, SS-9, SS-11 and SS-13, were already in development in the late 1950s. The deployment of SS-7 and SS-8 missiles did not get under way until 1962, but by the time Khrushchev left office the number of ICBMs deployed had risen to 224. The third-generation missiles were not deployed until 1965.

Towards a modern ICBM force

The fourth generation of Soviet ICBMs, consisting mostly of the highly accurate SS-19 with six warheads (360 missiles deployed) and the heavy SS 18 (308 missiles, mostly deployed in an eight- to ten-warhead configuration),[2] gave the Soviet Union a substantial counterforce capability against the United States and thus radically transformed the Soviet strategic nuclear force posture. Key advances were made in fuel technology (allowing the SS-17 and SS-18 to be cold-launched) and guidance systems (putting ICBM silos in the continental USA within reach of the SS-18 and SS-19). The development of MIRVs allowed a large expansion of the number of warheads deployed while keeping the number of launchers fixed as provided under the SALT I agreement. The mid-1970s also saw the deployment of SLBMs of intercontinental range.[3]

By comparison with US strategic forces, however, the Soviet

ICBM force still suffered from significant technological disadvantages. Although the storable fuels used for the propulsion systems allowed the missiles to be launched within a very short period (four to eight minutes), it would have been preferable to use solid fuels which allow launch at the turn of a key and also deliver more power for a given volume. Two early solid-fuel ICBM designs, the SS-13 and the SS-16, were not very successful. The SS-13 was deployed in small numbers and the SS-16 not at all. The principal constraint on the use of solid fuels appears to have been that their uneven rate of burn required the missile to be equipped with a highly accurate inertial guidance system. Since the Soviets still had considerable problems with their guidance systems, they found it necessary to rely on liquid fuels.[4]

The SS-18 (RS-20), codenamed Satan by NATO, is a very heavy missile and a successor to the SS-9. As its designation might indicate, this missile has been perceived by Western analysts as the most threatening element of the Soviet strategic arsenal. By the late 1970s, the fourth modification of the SS-18 was carrying ten MIRVed 0.55 megaton warheads while the accuracy had improved to 0.14 nautical miles. By 1980, 308 SS-18s were therefore in principle capable of delivering 3,080 warheads on the continental United States.

The SS-19 (RS-18), a liquid-fuel missile, is capable of carrying six 0.55 megaton MIRVed warheads or a 4.3 megaton single warhead; 350, mostly MIRVed (modification 3), were ultimately deployed. The SS-19, like the SS-11, is a missile of variable range and it has been estimated that 120 were deployed as regional weapons in the European and Far Eastern theatres, rather than as ICBMs. The SS-18 and the SS-19 were seen by Western analysts as the principal counterforce elements threatening the US Minuteman ICBM force.

The structure of the Soviet fourth-generation ICBM force (including the surviving elements of the third generation, the SS-11 and the SS-13) is such that it provides a versatile capability against a whole range of targets, including civilian and economic targets. It is quite evident none the less that the SS-18 and SS-19 force was designed to provide the capability to attack Minuteman silos. Hardened command-and-control centres were also likely targets for this force. Important soft targets in the continental United States, such as strategic bomber fields, military headquarters and countervalue targets,[5] could be handled by single-warhead SS-17 and SS-19 missiles. The SS-11 and the SS-18 were also suitable for attacking long-range naval targets.

The strategic force posture achieved by the end of the 1970s was in essence a partial achievement of the capabilities which Soviet spokesmen claimed they possessed during the 1960s. In line with the new Soviet thinking that in the event of war the escalation to the strategic nuclear level ought to be avoided, it was essentially a posture of deterrence. It was designed to guarantee an effective second-strike capability in order to safeguard Soviet territory. Hence the emphasis on reducing the vulnerability of ICBMs by hardening silos and developing reload facilities for cold-launched missiles, increasing rapid launch capabilities, and early warning facilities. In continuity with Soviet military thought since World War II, the primary orientation of Soviet targeting was counter-military.[6]

The emerging vulnerability of land-based ICBMs became one of the central issues of the strategic debate in the United States in the 1970s and 1980s. This became known as the 'window of vulnerability'. It was alleged that the Soviet Union would soon be able to take out the entire American ICBM force in a first strike. However, even the most pessimistic analyses acknowledged that the SS-18 and SS-19 were not accurate enough to give the Soviets sufficient confidence to launch such an attack. The claim rested principally on projected future capabilities. It also ignored the substantial second-strike capability of the relatively invulnerable American SLBM force. All the evidence seems to indicate that the Soviet Union was and remains deterred by US strategic nuclear power and that its own capabilities serve a deterrent function.

Nevertheless, the increasing capability of the Soviet Union to threaten the US ICBM force remains a fact which needs to be taken into account in American strategic calculations. More interesting from our point of view is whether the vulnerability of their own ICBMs was an important issue for the Soviet military. Although there are no direct indications of concern in the Soviet Union over ICBM vulnerability, the nature and direction of their fifth generation ICBM developments make it very clear: both the SS-24 and SS-25 were to be deployed in a mobile mode.

The fifth generation of Soviet ICBMs, which emerged in the 1980s, constitutes an important step towards a truly modern missile force measured by the standards of American technology. The first successful solid-fuelled missile deployed by the Soviet Union was the intermediate range SS-20. Both the SS-24 and SS-25 (RS-12M) are solid-fuelled, which is essential for a quick alert rate and for mobility. It is also clear that the Soviets have made important advances in inertial guidance systems. The accuracy of the SS-24 and SS-25 is given by the International Institute for Strategic Studies (IISS) as slightly better than that of the most accurate Minuteman III but not as good as the American MX missile.[7] The SS-24 is essentially the Soviet answer to the MX. Its throw-weight is estimated to be slightly higher than that of the MX, and like the MX it carries ten MIRVed warheads. In line with the current Soviet policy of ensuring invulnerability through mobility, the SS-24 is mounted on railway wagons. By June 1988 just ten SS-24s had been deployed. The SS-25 is a single-warhead missile which can be moved about by road. It is the Soviet counterpart to the American Midgetman missile. Deployment began in 1985, and about 100 SS-25s are now reckoned to have been deployed.

The general trends in the evolution of the Soviet strategic force posture during the 1980s can be summarized as follows:

(a) increasing progress in the mastery of the complex fuel and guidance technologies;
(b) reduced ICBM vulnerability through mobility;
(c) the emergence of a genuine triad with the development of an intercontinental range bomber, ALCMs and a modern long-range SLBM force.

These trends are based on the evolution of military technology and military-strategic logic alone. The influence of the new political thinking on strategic arms policy manifests itself primarily in discussion about minimum nuclear deterrence and the Soviet proposals for strategic arms reductions which will be discussed below.

Soviet strategic nuclear power at sea
The Soviet Union began deploying nuclear missiles on submarines in the late 1950s, first on the diesel-propelled Zulu and Golf, then on the nuclear-powered Hotel submarines. The SS-N-4 and SS-N-5 missiles developed by the Yangel bureau had a range of 350 and 750

nautical miles respectively and thus could only reach US territory after being deployed relatively close to the American coast. The SS-N-4 could only be fired if the submarine surfaced. Forward deployment of Hotel-class submarines equipped with SS-N-5s began in 1965. Even the third generation of SLBMs, the SS-N-6 deployed on Golf IV and Yankee I submarines in 1968, was not a missile of strategic range such as the American Polaris missile. According to Western experts, by 1970 the Soviets had deployed not more than forty-one SLBMs in a strategic mode.

The fourth generation SS-N-8, which first became operational in 1973, represented a quantum jump in Soviet SLBM development. It had a range of 4,200 nautical miles and was the first Soviet SLBM to use stellar inertial guidance. It was deployed on the Hotel III and the new Delta I and Delta II submarines. It was now possible for the Soviet Union to maintain a strategic reserve strike force that could inflict substantial damage on the continental United States from a much safer position closer to home waters. Nevertheless, the gap in technical capabilities between the Soviet Union and the United States was still greater with regard to SLBMs than to ICBMs. The Soviet SLBM programme slowly continued, and by 1978 the SS-N-18 was ready for deployment on the Delta III submarine; this modern, liquid-fuelled missile with three MIRVed warheads (later increased to seven) of 0.2 megaton had a range of 3,200 nautical miles. By 1980 the Soviet Union had deployed 522 SLBMs in a strategic mode. This represented less than 20% of all strategic warheads deployed by the Soviet Union, whereas the United States had more than 50% of all its warheads deployed on SLBMs.

A number of explanations have been advanced for this fundamental asymmetry. First of all, there is a strong naval tradition in the United States, whereas until recently the Soviet Union has been primarily a continental power. It is also evident that the Soviets had great difficulty in mastering the relevant technologies. Thus Soviet submarines are relatively noisy and consequently quite vulnerable to the extensive US ASW network, and the Soviets do not have the technical capabilities to locate and track the missile-carrying US submarines. The peacetime deployment rate for Soviet submarines is very low (of the order of 15% of submarines are on station at any given time, compared with 55% of the US submarines). It is also known that the Soviets are concerned about the command-and-control problems posed by submarines, including the dangers of unauthorized launch. One can therefore discern a whole nexus of problems which explain the Soviet bias for ICBMs.[8]

The Typhoon, which was first deployed in 1983, represents a further significant step forward in Soviet SLBM development and the creation of a relatively invulnerable but capable strategic nuclear reserve force. So far, five Typhoons which can carry twenty SS-N-20 missiles have been deployed. The SS-N-20 is a solid-fuelled missile with ten MIRVed warheads. A further development is the SS-N-23 missile with four warheads, first deployed in 1986 on Delta IV submarines. Although still vulnerable to American ASW, the Typhoon is a much quieter submarine than its predecessors. Its development is in part a response to the Trident programme and signals – apart from the strategic rationales for a sea-based strategic reserve[9] – the determination of the Soviet military planners to close the gap with the United States in all areas of military technology.

Soviet strategic forces: future prospects

Official Soviet policy has long advocated ending the nuclear arms race. As we have seen, already under Brezhnev the Soviet leadership had accepted a state of mutual vulnerability and the impossibility of contemplating first strike. The general shift in military policy under Gorbachev was particularly obvious in strategic arms policy. This is an area where it appeared possible to make drastic arms reductions, potentially of high symbolic significance, without affecting military capabilities in the most likely conflicts that might arise. The hallmark of the new policy was a more serious endeavour to achieve the long-stated Soviet goal of total nuclear disarmament, and on 15 January 1986 Gorbachev proposed the total elimination of all nuclear weapons by the year 2000.[10]

This was given more substance at the Reykjavik summit in October 1986, when Gorbachev proposed a 50% cut in intercontinental strategic weapons within five years and their total elimination within ten years. Since then, considerable progress on a START agreement has been made, which may lead to a cut of 30% of warheads on ballistic missiles (using the counting rules developed for START).

Although the official goal of total nuclear disarmament has not been abandoned, there is some scepticism as to whether this is a realistic objective, and in recent years much work has been done in the academic institutes on interim goals for minimum deterrence or nuclear sufficiency. Since 1984 the Committee of Soviet Scientists for Peace Against the Nuclear Threat, supervised by Academician Roald Sagdeev, Director of the Institute for Space Research, and Andrei Kokoshin, Deputy Director of ISKAN, have been engaged in studies of various modes of drastic strategic arms reduction. The central concept is that of strategic stability. The scholars engaged in this research prepared assessments of various configurations of force postures based on extensive computer modelling. The fundamental criterion of stability was the possibility of carrying out a completely or partially disarming first strike, with stability decreasing as one side increased its first-strike potential. The precise means whereby counterforce first-strike capabilities are evaluated has not been explained in detail, but it is evident from the published reports that they take into account a whole variety of factors including the precise mix of forces, damage limitation measures, strategic defences, etc., and were worked out for quite a number of different possible situations.[11] Not surprisingly, an unlimited arms race in the future was linked with a linear decrease in stability.

Of particular interest are the following: the US START proposals of 1987, the Soviet START proposals of 1987, and 'the scrapping and prohibition of further deployment of counterforce systems, and switching over to mobile-based single-warhead delivery systems'.[12] All of these schemes would have resulted, according to this model, in significant increases in stability over time, with the last one showing a considerably more rapid increase than the others. As it turns out, this indicates one of the policy preferences for strategic arms control current in the Soviet arms control community.

To arrive at a concept of minimum deterrence, the Soviet arms control community has taken up a Western concept – namely, the potential to inflict unacceptable damage in a retaliatory strike. This is called the McNamara (or M) index. According to Aleksei Arbatov:

> The threshold of unacceptable damage deduced by US Defense Secretary Robert McNamara in the 1960s is the destruction of about 70 percent of industrial potential and 30 percent of the population. Such a destruction requires approximately 400 nuclear warheads of the megaton class; so the M-index is the aggregate equivalent megatonnage divided by the number 400.[13]

Strategic arms policy

There has evidently been some disagreement as to whether a McNamara index of 1 represents minimum deterrence. Arbatov himself and a number of other specialists consider the McNamara threshold 'absurdly high', if all the secondary effects of 400 nuclear strikes of 1 megaton on the Soviet Union are taken into account. But Arbatov reports that in view of the large number of industrial and military targets in the Soviet Union and the United States, some strategists take the view that the McNamara index of 1 may not be sufficient to cover all the targets that need to be covered for effective minimum deterrence. The scheme of minimum deterrence advocated by the Committee proposes that each of the superpowers should retain 600 mobile single-warhead ICBMs (McNamara index of 1.5) and scrap all their other strategic nuclear forces. Furthermore, it advocates that strategic defences should not be deployed, as its mathematical models appear to show that they are destabilizing. Much emphasis is put on whether command and control facilities can survive.

This preference for ICBMs as leading to a more stable strategic environment is in stark contrast to the American view, which has seen ballistic missiles as the central factor of instability. US arms control efforts (particularly in the post-Reykjavik phase of START) have been directed at reducing or even eliminating ICBM forces. The arguments put forward by the Soviet academics for the stabilizing character of unMIRVed ICBMs are as follows:

(a) Command and control of ICBMs is much more reliable. Two-way communication with submarines may at times be disrupted and therefore requires that submarine crews must technically be able to fire missiles without authorization.

(b) The trajectories of ICBMs are relatively predictable after launch and therefore facilitate early warning. SLBMs and particularly SLCMs are much more suitable for attempts to bypass early warning systems.

(c) Although ICBMs have come to be considered the most effective counterforce weapons, the accuracy of SLBMs has now improved considerably. By restricting the force to mobile single-warhead ICBMs both the vulnerability and the first-strike potential problem can be overcome, since it takes more than one warhead targeted per enemy missile to be assured of a successful first strike, and this in any event becomes virtually impossible if the missiles are mobile.

(d) As a delivery vehicle for nuclear weapons, bombers are not considered conducive to a stable strategic environment because of their nuclear/conventional dual capability.

More recently, Aleksei Arbatov has taken his ideas a step further and has made some proposals for the direction Soviet strategic arms policy could take independent of arms control. Again, he takes a strong line against counterforce targeting. The role of nuclear forces in his view is not war-fighting (defeating the armed forces of the aggressor) or damage limitation, but to threaten a crushing retaliatory counterstrike against the vital centres of the enemy's homeland. Another dominant feature of his approach seems to be the cutting-back of very expensive new programmes which do not appear to enhance Soviet security sufficiently to justify their cost. In terms of strategic programmes, he makes the following recommendations:

(a) As both ICBM vulnerability and MIRVs (which are part and parcel of a first-strike capability) are destabilizing, the Soviet Union should proceed with the deployment of the SS-25 but scrap the ten-warhead SS-24.
(b) Scrap the large Typhoon submarine programme and deploy SLBMs on the smaller Delta IV.
(c) Scrap the TU-160 aircraft (Blackjack). Its missions should continue to be assigned to the old TU-95 (Bear), or a new high capacity aircraft should be developed to carry ALCMs.
(d) Only one of the two SLCMs currently being developed (the SS-N-21 and SS-N-24) should be continued and deployed.
(e) The ABM system around Moscow should be dismantled, along with a substantial part of the enormous but ineffective Soviet air defence system; only battlefield air defence and a minimal system for early warning should be retained.[14]

Arbatov's most recent proposals have drawn criticism from military leaders, who make it clear that they are not prepared to contemplate such drastic restructuring of the Soviet strategic nuclear forces.[15]

The scheme for nuclear sufficiency worked out by the arms control specialists has been criticized in the journal *International Affairs* by three writers from the Ministry for Foreign Affairs,

S. Vybornov, A. Gusenkov and V. Leontiev. They criticize the fundamental premise that mobile ICBMs are particularly conducive to stability. The central issue is whether soft mobile basing instead of hard fixed silo basing makes them more vulnerable, and whether, given the accuracy of state-of-the-art guidance systems and the extent of satellite reconnaissance capabilities, mobility can really yield the degree of invulnerability that can be achieved by submarine basing. Indeed, they suggest that a first strike could be conducted with conventional precision-guided munitions, thus lowering the risk of such a venture and creating a less stable environment.

The Foreign Ministry authors also criticize Arbatov and his colleagues for not taking into account third countries' systems. They differ from them in their attitude to total nuclear disarmament (which they do not consider ultimately desirable). They do not assume that third-power arsenals can be eliminated by arms control. At the same time their assumption is that these countries would be included in the arms control process. Their version of minimum deterrence assumes submarine basing restricted to certain well-defined patrol regions. Each of these regions is to be limited to submarines carrying SLBMs with up to 300 warheads and is to remain free of anti-submarine warfare (ASW) forces. Each of the superpowers is to be allowed two patrol regions, and third forces (China and a joint Anglo-French force) are to be allowed one patrol zone. There are naturally a host of problems with this scheme, related to the precise definition of the patrol zones, the overall balance of forces between the United States, the Soviet Union and other nuclear powers, and verification. Nevertheless it is significant as an illustration of variety in approaches to nuclear sufficiency being proposed in the Soviet Union.[16]

There is little evidence that these studies of nuclear sufficiency are having much influence on Soviet strategic arms policy or on the Soviet position at the START negotiations. The configuration of Soviet strategic forces over the coming decade will therefore probably depend principally on whether a START agreement is concluded and what its final shape will be. In the absence of arms control, it can be expected that ICBM modernization would continue. The older ICBMs would gradually be phased out, with the SS-24s, the SS-25s, the SS-18 (modification 5) and perhaps some SS-19s remaining. CIA estimates indicate that in the next decade about one-third of Soviet land-based warheads will be on mobile ICBMs.

Strategic arms policy

The modernization of the sea-based forces would continue, with the older, noisier submarines being phased out and SLBMs being based primarily on Delta II, Delta III and Typhoon submarines. They would be deployed by preference out of reach of US ASW forces, close to the Soviet mainland. Since even the Typhoon is still noisy by US standards, it is a plausible assumption that the mid-1990s would see another new design more capable of evading US ASW networks. According to CIA estimates the Soviet Union may deploy as many as 1,500 SLCMs by the mid-1990s. It is unlikely that this is a preferred option. It is probably intended to come into play only if no progress on SLCMs is made in START.

The Soviet strategic bomber force, until now the most neglected leg of the Soviet strategic triad, could well come into its own. It is a fair assumption that the most up-to-date version of the Bear, the Bear-H, and the new Blackjack would constitute most of the growing bomber force. At present, the Bear-H is equipped to carry six AS-15 ALCMs, but its capacity could be increased to carry another four. The Blackjack is being equipped with twenty-four SRAMs but it could carry twelve ALCMs instead. It is not clear whether a dramatic increase in the size of the bomber fleet is planned. The modernization programme has, however, resulted in a sharp rise in the number of warheads carried on strategic bombers, which may reach 2,000 by the mid-1990s.[17]

For Soviet and American arms negotiators the impact of START on Soviet deployment patterns is therefore of critical significance. There has been agreement so far on the following constraints in a future START agreement:

(a) The total number of delivery vehicles deployed (ICBMs, SLBMs and heavy bombers) is to be limited to 1,600.

(b) The total number of warheads deployed is to be limited to 6,000, with a sublimit of 4,900 on ballistic missiles (ICBMs and SLBMs) and of 1,540 on heavy missiles (only the SS-18 currently counts as a heavy missile).

(c) Under the counting rules agreed for the 6,000 ceiling, each warhead on a ballistic missile counts as one, as does the entire load of gravity bombs or SRAMs carried on a heavy bomber.

The following are the principal areas that remain to be resolved:

(a) The United States has proposed a sublimit of 3,300 warheads deployed on ICBMs. Although the Soviet negotiators have indicated that there is no intention to exceed this sublimit in any event, they would only accept it if a similar sublimit were to be placed on SLBM limits, even further constraining the 'freedom to mix'. This has been rejected by the United States.

(b) No counting rules have been agreed for ALCMs. The Soviet position has been to assume that each bomber will carry the maximum number possible. As the United States plans to deploy substantially less than the maximum technically possible, it is seeking a reduction in the number of ALCMs for each bomber.

(c) The United States proposed a ban on mobile ICBMs, primarily on account of the difficulty of verification. As Soviet ICBM modernization is entirely oriented towards mobility, this proposal has been rejected. Although there has been a significant shift in the American position on this issue, it remains subject to debate within the United States (the administration is unwilling to agree to the deployment of mobile ICBMs unless there is funding for an American mobile ICBM). The problem remains to be resolved.

(d) No agreement has been reached on SLCMs. The Soviet side has proposed a limit of 400 nuclear-tipped SLCMs on two classes of submarines and 600 conventional SLCMs on certain designated types of ships, or in order to meet objections about verification a combined limit of 1,000 on nuclear and conventional SLCMs. The American position remains that SLCMs should not be dealt with under START.[18]

(e) There is some interest among American arms control experts, the most influential among them being Senator Sam Nunn, to encourage de-MIRVing in START and to ban MIRVed mobile missiles. This would amount to trading off the MX against the SS-24. As is clear from the discussion above, some Soviet arms control experts would favour de-MIRVing. Technical difficulties with the SS-24 might encourage Soviet receptiveness to such a proposal. How these debates will be resolved either in Moscow or Washington is not clear at the time of writing, however.

START would require the Soviet Union to cut the number of its delivery vehicles by over 35%. Given the view prevalent in both superpowers that the Soviet Union is most advanced in weapons technology with regard to ICBMs, the most likely result of START would be to reduce the Soviet SLBM force substantially. This would contradict the American goal in the early phases of the talks of 'pushing the Soviets out to sea'. At the same time, most of the older ICBMs would probably be scrapped, with only SS-19s, SS-18s and the fifth generation missiles remaining in service. START would therefore serve to promote the modernization of the Soviet ICBM force. The wild card in the pack will be the bombers. START counting rules would encourage an increased deployment of strategic bombers while discouraging the deployment of ALCMs. Given the technical difficulties of the Blackjack and the traditional bias of the Soviets towards ICBMs, it is uncertain to what extent they plan to develop their strategic bomber fleet.[19]

In general, however, the START process does seem to offer a more realistic hope of achieving significant reductions and a more stable strategic environment. Britain and France, of course, are currently excluded from the talks. It is clear that this must change if arms control is to continue after START.

5
SOVIET STRATEGIC DEFENCE

The Strategic Defence Initiative launched by President Reagan in March 1983 had the effect of bringing the issue of strategic defence back into the forefront of the arms control process from which it had been virtually absent since the signing of the ABM Treaty in 1972. It also put the question of Soviet views and capabilities in the realm of ballistic missile defence at the centre of political debate.

Soviet strategic defence played a paradoxical role in the Western debate about SDI. President Reagan presented his initiative as a new vision to be realized by radical technological breakthroughs. The fruits of this massive research programme were then to be shared with the Soviets so as to enhance the security of both sides. Others, notably Defence Secretary Caspar Weinberger and his deputy Richard Perle, claimed that the Soviet Union had a very substantial programme of strategic defence based on conventional as well as new technologies and that therefore an American response was required. These contradictory justifications made for an inconsistent approach to the role of SDI in arms control. The logical consequence of the Weinberger/Perle approach would be to question the Soviet commitment to the ABM Treaty and seek to strengthen either the provisions of the Treaty or the means of monitoring compliance with it. This, however, ran counter to the general attitude prevailing in the Department of Defence on the role of arms control. Europeans, on the other hand, saw SDI as a bargaining chip in arms control, to be used to contain a Soviet strategic defence 'breakout'.

Soviet strategic defence

But if the purpose of SDI was to make offensive nuclear weapons 'impotent and obsolete', then it had no place in arms control.

One fundamental issue which played an important role in these debates was the Soviet attitude to strategic defence. Many of those who supported SDI as a response to Soviet efforts in the field of ballistic missile defence expressed the conviction that the Soviet Union merely signed the ABM Treaty to forestall American BMD at a time when the United States had a technological advantage, that Soviet support for the ABM Treaty did not signal a definite renunciation of strategic defence and the acceptance of mutual vulnerability, and that the Soviets had been engaged in a major effort to develop new BMD capabilities for a long time. According to this view, the Soviets were intending to build a substantial national ballistic missile defence system when military technology rendered this advantageous, so as to enhance their ability to fight a nuclear war. There was much argument over how to interpret Soviet motivations in first developing strategic defences and then accepting the limitations on ballistic missile defence in the ABM Treaty. A brief historical review is therefore in order.

The origins of BMD in the Soviet Union and the ABM Treaty

Defence of the USSR against attack from the air is the domain of the branch of the military services known as PVO-S (*Protivovozdushnaya Oborona Strany* – anti-air defence of the country). The PVO became a separate major component of the armed forces in 1955 after a substantial reorganization of the air defence system.

The effort of the 1950s to develop an effective system of defence against air attack had two main components: first, to provide capable interceptor fighters; and, second, to develop surface-to-air missiles with which to defend the Soviet Union against the threat from the growing American intercontinental bomber force. The technology of surface-to-air missiles apparently became available to the Soviet Union in 1952.[1] The first missiles were deployed in 1956 around Moscow. The SAM-1 was not deployed elsewhere, presumably on account of deficiencies in performance. The SAM-2 became available in 1958. This high-altitude missile was responsible for the spectacularly successful downing of the U2 spy plane in May 1960, an event which had a significant influence on East-West relations at the time. The SAM-2 was widely deployed throughout the Soviet

Soviet strategic defence

Union and Eastern Europe, and was later used in North Vietnam against American bombers.

The next logical step was to develop a defence against the ICBM threat which began to emerge in the late 1950s. Already in 1957 there were signs that the Soviet Union was contemplating the deployment of an anti-ballistic missile system.[2] US intelligence observed one or two large radar systems which, judging by their size and location, appeared not to be connected with the air defence system. The suggestion that the Russians might be experimenting with ballistic missile defence was based on comparisons with the kind of radars that were being studied for a possible American ABM development.[3]

In 1958, the air defence command was reorganized in anticipation of ABM deployment. The command was split into the PSO (*Protivo-Samoletnaya Oborona* – anti-aircraft defence) and the PRO (*Protivo-Raketnaya Oborona* – anti-rocket defence). By 1960, it appears, the development of an operational ABM system had assumed some degree of importance for the Soviet leadership. At the 22nd CPSU Congress Defence Minister Marshal Malinovsky declared that 'the problem of destroying missiles in flight ... has been successfully solved'.[4] Then a few months before the Cuban missile crisis, in July 1962, Khrushchev made his famous remark about having at his disposal missiles which could 'hit a fly in outer space'.[5]

The reason for all this optimism was the deployment around Leningrad in 1962 of the SAM-5 missile, codenamed Griffon by Western intelligence. The policy on missile defence resembled somewhat Khrushchev's approach to ICBM development. There was general support for a limited ABM programme, about which there was a great deal of boasting. On the other hand, resources for the determined development of a ballistic missile defence system that might even be modestly effective were not made available. A second-generation ABM intended for deployment around Moscow, codenamed Galosh by NATO, was shown on Red Square three weeks after the fall of Khrushchev, on 7 November 1964.

Ballistic missile defence was very controversial in the Soviet Union. Most of the military establishment – the PVO excluded – favoured channelling resources towards ICBMs instead. The reason was in part the technical difficulties of the ABM system. It was not clear that greater allocation of resources would in fact produce an effective ballistic missile defence, while greater investment in ICBM production seemed likely to give a guaranteed return.[6] Second, the institutional interests of other military services, in particular the Ground Forces and the Strategic Rocket Forces, conflicted strongly with a substantially increased allocation of resources for the development of strategic defence. So far as strategic doctrine is concerned, the primacy of strategic, offensive missile forces was clearly affirmed in the first two editions of the Sokolovsky work *Voennaya strategiya*, published in 1962 and 1963. The strategic argument in favour of the development and deployment of a strategic defence system was advanced in October 1964 by Major-General Nikolai Talensky, a prominent military historian in the Soviet Academy of Sciences, in the journal *International Affairs*. This article, together with early statements by Khrushchev and Malinovsky, are still frequently quoted to demonstrate Soviet doctrinal support for BMD. A closer analysis of the Soviet debate at the time shows that there was significant disagreement on this issue and that the professional military by and large did not favour increased investment in BMD. One of its most outspoken opponents was the Chief of the General Staff, Matvei Zakharov. It is clear that by 1966 the ABM programme was given a significantly reduced priority. Public statements by representatives of the military establishment indicate a more realistic assessment of what an ABM system, pursued within present technological capabilities and a likely investment of resources, could and could not do.[7]

The decline of strategic defence and the ABM Treaty

The debate continued well into 1967, when it became part of the emerging SALT process. In January 1967 President Johnson asked Llewellyn E. Thompson, who was returning to Moscow for a second term as ambassador, to explore the possibility of negotiations to limit ABM deployment. The response by Thompson's counterpart Dobrynin indicated Soviet interest in such negotiations provided that offensive forces were also included. In a public speech Kosygin seemed to pour cold water on the idea of limiting ballistic missile defence. The position of the Soviet leadership, however, including Kosygin (as a close analysis of his public statement reveals), was not that there should be no limitations on ABMs, but rather that such limitations could only be accepted in a general framework that also limited offensive weapons. For a time, the Galosh programme continued under its own momentum. The first launch positions were installed by 1967. In late 1968 work on the Moscow system came to a complete halt, however, having been about two-thirds completed.

It is clear that already in 1967 the PVO and the ABM programme in particular were steadily losing support in the Soviet military. The reasons were first of all the realization that the Galosh system would not provide a satisfactory defence against an American ICBM attack and indeed a general disillusionment with regard to the system's capabilities; second, the growth in the Soviet offensive arsenal, which encouraged an increased emphasis on offensive forces; and third, the realization that the American Nike-X ABM system was in fact superior to the Soviet one. More important than constraining US BMD was, however, the development of MIRVed missiles which further diminished the credibility of ballistic missile defence.[8] Of symbolic significance was the fact that for the first time since 1963 the November military parade in 1968 did not feature any ABM devices (nor did any subsequent parades).

Raymond Garthoff, executive officer of the US delegation to the SALT talks from 1969 to 1973, has described the head of the Soviet delegation's initial presentation on the ABM issue in the following terms:

> In one of the first formal SALT meetings, in November 1969, Deputy Minister Vladimir Semenov, the head of the Soviet delegation, set forth the Soviet position on ABM limitation. He acknowledged indirectly the change in Soviet views by saying that, although initially it had seemed that ABM would serve humane goals and that the only problem seemed to be a technical one, it was later found that ABM systems could stimulate the arms race and could be destabilizing by casting doubts on the inevitability of effective retaliation by missile forces of the side attacked. In view of the strategic defensive-offensive interrelationship, ABM deployment could be strategically destabilizing.[9]

While Galosh deployment came to a halt in late 1968, a high level of research in ballistic missile defence continued and work on the uncompleted Moscow site started again in 1971. However, the Soviet leadership had come to the conclusion that it was more advantageous to negotiate an agreement abandoning further Soviet BMD deployment and thus preventing the deployment of the

Soviet strategic defence

technologically superior American ABM system, than to extend the Galosh system throughout the Soviet Union. In signing the ABM Treaty in 1972, the Soviet Union, like the US, accepted a ceiling of 200 ABM launchers, which was reduced to 100 in a further agreement in June 1974, thus bringing to a conclusion for the time being the Soviet debate about ballistic missile defence.

Soviet ballistic missile defence after the ABM Treaty
After the signing of the ABM Treaty, discussion of ballistic missile defence virtually disappeared from the open military press. The journal of the air defence troops confined its attention to anti-aircraft defence, even though the Moscow ABM system continued to operate under the aegis of the PVO. The only body of evidence that yields any clues about Soviet thinking consists in the observed development and deployment of systems. Whereas the United States dismantled all its ABM launchers of the Safeguard system, the Soviet Union maintained the Moscow system and undertook a long-term development programme to upgrade it. This finally came to fruition in 1980 when the capabilities of the system were substantially improved within the limits of the ABM Treaty. Thirty-two of the old Galosh launchers were dismantled and new, more advanced missiles deployed, their number increased to the permitted ceiling of 100. Another important component of the modernization programme was the construction of the new pill-boxed large phased-array radar system at Pushkino, which made the simultaneous interception of a number of incoming missiles a more feasible prospect. The modernized Soviet ABM system around Moscow (referred to as ABM-3-X) is roughly equivalent in technological terms to the US Safeguard system and provides a limited defence against hostile missile launches. Thus the system could be expected to perform well against the very limited Chinese strategic missile force. American, and even French and British, strategic forces are well capable of saturating and penetrating the Moscow defences. The radar system is an obviously vulnerable point – one direct hit or high-altitude nuclear detonations generating a large electromagnetic pulse could disable the entire system. The British Chevaline warhead for the Polaris system was specifically designed to overcome the Moscow defences.

The continuation of the Moscow ABM system reflects the priority given to protecting the national capital. It thus could be said to vindicate the 'Moscow criterion' for British strategic forces.[10] But there has been no determined attempt to upgrade this protection to a high level. It bears all the hallmarks of an existing programme continuing under its own momentum, rather than a shift in the role of strategic missile defence.

Nevertheless, in the early 1980s a number of commentators raised fears that the Soviet Union might be preparing a 'breakout' from the ABM Treaty, deploying a nationwide ABM system. These fears were based on two principal areas of concern: the upgrading of surface-to-air missiles and improvements in Soviet radar capabilities. The issue of upgrading surface-to-air missiles deployed against the US strategic bomber threat to ABMs played an important role in the SALT I negotiations. In the 1960s, there was much debate within the US administration about the possible BMD capability of the SA-5 missile, which in the end was judged to be marginal at best. More recently, the SA-10 and the SA-X-12 have come under similar scrutiny. The SA-10 became operational in 1980 and about 800 SA-10 launchers have been deployed, more than half in the Moscow district. The SA-10 is believed by the US Department of Defense to have some effectiveness against cruise missiles and possibly against SLBMs, which fly at a slower speed than ICBMs and have a larger radar cross-section. Unlike the SA-5, the SA-10 has never been tested in an ABM mode, and any ballistic missile defence capability attributed to the SA-10 is thus theoretical. The SA-X-12 has been tested in an anti-tactical ballistic missile role (ATBM mode) against the SS-12 with limited success.[11]

There has also been some concern about Soviet radar installations. A long-standing issue in arms control compliance has been the testing of radars for the SA-5 in an ABM mode. This issue was largely resolved in the SALT Standing Consultative Commission. But modern Soviet air defence radar capabilities have given rise to further concerns.[12] There is apprehension that by upgrading its surface-to-air missile capacity, which is based on a large number of air defence missiles, the Soviet Union will be able at some point to break out of the ABM Treaty restrictions. The best-known symbol of concern over Soviet strategic defence capabilities is the radar installation at Abalakovo in Krasnoyarsk. The ABM Treaty allows early-warning phased array radars to be built only facing upward on the periphery of the United States and the Soviet Union. Such

Soviet strategic defence

limitations do not apply to phased-array radars designed for space-tracking. The Krasnoyarsk radar was sited deep inside Soviet territory (about 500 miles from the Mongolian border), was facing inward and was not far to the north and northeast of SS-18 ICBM fields. These circumstances gave rise to claims in the United States that the Krasnoyarsk installation was an ABM battle management radar and violated the ABM Treaty.

The first of these assertions was dubious, given that the entry path for US ICBM re-entry vehicles coming over the North Pole towards the ICBM fields was not in fact covered by the Krasnoyarsk radar. Furthermore, there were no missiles deployed that could have been directed by the radar information to intercept incoming ICBMs. A British intelligence study claimed that the radar was designed for space-tracking purposes and was thus not in violation of the ABM Treaty. This conclusion, which is in conformity with Soviet explanations of the purpose of the radar, has been widely disputed. It seems that the radar was to have been part of a chain of modern LPARS (large phased-array radars), all, except for the Krasnoyarsk radar, sited along the borders of the Soviet Union. The Krasnoyarsk radar was never completed and will now be dismantled in response to the allegations of treaty violations. In a final intriguing twist to the Krasnoyarsk saga, Soviet Foreign Minister Eduard Shevardnadze publicly admitted that the radar constituted a violation of the ABM Treaty and that the Soviet military experts had misled the civilian government on this matter. It is evident, however, that while the LPAR network could support ballistic missile defence, the Krasnoyarsk radar was never designed to enable Soviet breakout from the ABM Treaty.

The final area of concern has been Soviet research into exotic BMD technologies. Particular attention has been paid to Soviet research into lasers, particle beams, space platforms and anti-satellite systems. There is no doubt that research and development of lasers is being intensively pursued in the Soviet Union, for a whole range of different applications. There has been some discussion of the use of laser systems for BMD purposes in the Soviet literature. The Department of Defence claimed in 1986 that two ground-based laser installations had been built at Sary Shagan (a launching site for ASAT), possibly intended to provide a capability to blind the sensors of US satellites. The evidence available so far indicates, however, that Soviet laser technology is not in advance of that in the

United States, and no systems have been developed with a definite capability for a role in strategic defence.[13] Furthermore, the usefulness of laser systems in ballistic missile defence has been generally exaggerated. In the latter years of the Strategic Defence Initiative, the role of laser weapons (in particular space-based systems) has declined dramatically, given the technical difficulties of using lasers to destroy targets at long range, particularly if they are still in the atmosphere. X-ray lasers may still be considered for such a role, but this seems to be an area in which the relevant technological breakthroughs have been made in the United States, not the Soviet Union.

Research in the field of high-energy pulsed electron beams has been carried out by some of the major Academy of Sciences institutes in the Soviet Union since the early 1960s, including the Kurchatov Institute of Atomic Energy and the Lebedev Physics Institute in Moscow as well as the Nuclear Physics Institute in Novosibirsk. A large number of secondary institutions have also been involved, and despite the fact that the work at various institutions has been very diverse and under different administrative authorities, some US analysts have expressed the conviction that it is well coordinated. Much of this work also has civil applications, in the field of nuclear fusion research, but some US intelligence reports have stressed the military potential. This is supported by the observation that some of the research is under direct control of the PVO. In 1977 there was a report that a charged particle-beam research complex, with an estimated value of between $10 and $15 billion, was in operation in Soviet Central Asia, near Semipalatinsk. Another research facility in particle-beam technology was claimed to have been detected at Azgir in Kazakhstan near the Caspian Sea. The CIA has responded with scepticism to these claims. Nevertheless, during a visit to the Lawrence Livermore laboratories in California Soviet scientist Leonid Rudakov claimed that the Soviet Union had developed a technique to convert the energy from electron beams to compress fusionable material and release high fusion energy.

For all the excitement about such exotic technologies, it is still very unclear at the theoretical level whether particle-beam weapons will work. Neither in the Soviet Union nor anywhere else have particle-beam weapons been built, nor has the technology reached a state where weapons development could even begin. Furthermore, the Soviet Union has no significant technological advantage over the United States in this area.

The final area of concern is the military space programme. By steadily pouring in resources over a long period of time, the Soviet Union has developed unmanned lifting capabilities and space platforms which far exceed the US operational level. The Soviets have also accumulated much experience in manned orbital space stations and keeping people in space for long periods of time. Nevertheless, from a purely technological point of view, the United States is well capable of matching the Soviet Union, which relies on the adaptation of relatively crude technology. The Soviet space shuttle, for example, has yet to become fully operational. So far as military applications are concerned, the Soviet Union has developed, tested and deployed only a crude anti-satellite system which is capable of eliminating American low-orbit satellites. Only a small proportion of American satellites are within the range of the system, and to destroy all of those would take at least a week. American anti-satellite weapons (so-called miniature homing vehicles, i.e. missiles based on F-15 fighter aircraft), although they have not as yet been deployed, are potentially much more effective and capable.

Two principal conclusions emerge. The first is that although there has been some research effort in classical and exotic ballistic missile defence technologies, and the Soviet Union possesses the world's only deployed ABM and ASAT systems, it does not have the means, either in practice or in principle, to reduce the strategic missile threat that it faces from the United States, Britain and France, nor will it have in the foreseeable future. The second is that although the Soviet Union has significant advantage in some of the technologies for BMD, in nearly all the crucial areas of technology – missile propulsion, inertial guidance, radar sensing devices, microelectronics, computer technology, materials, robotics, electronic signal processing – the United States is ahead. Compared to American military systems, the Soviet equivalent is almost invariably much less technologically advanced. This technological disadvantage, as we shall see, was highly significant for the Soviet response to SDI.

The Soviet Union and SDI
The Soviet reaction to the Strategic Defence Initiative announced by President Reagan in March 1983 was marked by the same paradoxi-

cal features as the debate in the West: doubts were cast on its feasibility, yet it was simultaneously characterized as a very threatening and dangerous development. The Soviet literature is inconsistent about the technical feasibility of SDI, but in general it can be said that Soviet analysts began by stressing the enormous difficulties associated with a ballistic missile defence system that is to provide reliable area defence, while acknowledging the possible application of exotic technologies and space-based weapons in an ABM role within one or two decades. As time passed, however, doubts about the feasibility of SDI came to be expressed more strongly. Soviet experts, like their Western counterparts, had a field day, analysing the difficulties associated with the use of space-based chemical laser systems, particle beams, etc. Political analysts discussed at length the possible countermeasures to space-based strategic defence: a build-up in offensive systems to saturate the defence, increasing reliance on cruise missiles and SLBMs, coating missiles with materials which absorb the energy from laser beams without destroying the missile, reducing the boost phase to make missiles less vulnerable to attack, using smokescreens to mask missile launches, space mines to attack the space-based ballistic-missile defence platforms, and so on. It was not very difficult to demonstrate that the transition from an offence-dominated world to a defence-dominated world would be extremely difficult to achieve and easy to sabotage.

Given that the entire SDI programme was very vulnerable to such critiques, why was it perceived as so threatening? The initial Soviet view of SDI was as part of a general threat emerging from the policies of the Reagan administration. The development of new counterforce systems on strategic missiles (the MX ICBM and the Trident D5 SLBM), and the deployment of GLCMs and Pershing II missiles in Europe, plus the accompanying rhetoric about prevailing in a nuclear conflict, were seen as evidence of a sustained effort to develop a first-strike capability against the Soviet Union. SDI fitted perfectly into this picture, since its most likely practical implementation was to provide protection for American ICBM silos. This fear was clearly expressed by Yury Andropov in his interview with the German news magazine *Spiegel* when he said, 'the adventurism and danger of this entire venture is that they are counting on delivering a nuclear first strike with impunity, believing that they can protect themselves against a retaliatory strike. From here it is not far to the temptation to push the button.'[14]

This almost certainly overstates Soviet assessments of the dangers arising from SDI. Nevertheless there was a clear perception in the Soviet Union that under the guise of 'catching up' the United States was pushing to convert its military power into substantial political gains vis-à-vis the Soviet Union, by creating a convincing impression that it could successfully wage nuclear war. In the short term, it was evident that there was no military-technical threat from SDI. It threatened to block permanently the arms control process and to set the United States on a course for seeking unilateral military solutions. Furthermore, the United States was thought to be deliberately accelerating the military competition with the Soviet Union in order to bankrupt the Soviet economy. A common anxiety expressed in Soviet commentaries was that the *perception* of a functional strategic defence would be dangerous, since it would induce the other side to incur greater risks than it would otherwise be prepared to accept. In the long term, it could force the Soviet Union into a costly arms race in space and destabilize the strategic balance.

The advent of Gorbachev in 1985 only served to harden Soviet opposition to SDI. Indeed, stopping SDI then became one of the principal objectives of Soviet arms control policy. All of the far-reaching arms control endeavours were in some way linked to banning SDI. The unilateral test moratorium was a direct attempt to undermine SDI as well as to stop the further development of offensive nuclear weapons. Deep reductions in strategic offensive weapons were proposed subject to a ban on SDI. At the same time, the Soviet Union stressed the negative effect for East-West relations of proceeding with SDI.

The Geneva summit appeared to destroy any hope that progress could be made along the lines proposed by Gorbachev. Despite the improving atmosphere in East-West relations and an increasing desire for movement in the arms control area on both sides, President Reagan's commitment to SDI proved unshakeable. The only area of potential progress was INF (Intermediate Nuclear Forces) where the Soviet Union seemed willing to move ahead regardless of SDI.

In 1986 Gorbachev continued to push for progress in arms control and an improvement in Soviet-US relations. On 15 January he proposed complete nuclear disarmament by the year 2000. Real progress was made in the area of INF, where the insistence on the inclusion of British and French forces in an INF agreement was abandoned and the concept of a double zero INF agreement was accepted. In May 1986, Gorbachev elaborated his proposal for arms reductions in the area from the Atlantic to the Urals, and new Soviet proposals on chemical weapons were made. By now it had become clear that SDI was an obstacle to progress in arms control that could not be removed without some shift in the intransigent position of both sides.

The new Soviet approach which emerged by the end of May 1986 was more politically adept. Instead of demanding a ban on SDI, it called for measures to strengthen the ABM Treaty. In this way the Soviet Union could increase the political price of SDI for the Reagan administration, while at the same time opening up avenues for face-saving compromises on both sides. A less rigid attitude to linkage with SDI allowed for a great deal of progress on START and INF.

The Reykjavik summit in November 1986 demonstrated that both Gorbachev and Reagan were serious about substantial strategic arms reductions. At the same time SDI remained a serious obstacle to progress in arms control. The SDI/INF linkage was apparently reintroduced at Reykjavik, but this, as it turned out, was just the beginning of a process where the Soviet Union and the United States staked out their positions as to what level of activity on SDI would ultimately be acceptable. At Reykjavik Gorbachev appeared to insist that all SDI research and development would have to be restricted to the laboratory. But some confusion remained and some Soviet commentaries seemed to suggest that only the testing in space of actual identifiable components of a space-based defence system would not be permissible.[15]

Soviet ambiguity on this point continued until September 1987. In April 1987, for example, Gorbachev made a statement that appeared to widen the permissibility of tests outside the confines of a laboratory building to anywhere other than in space. At the same time he proposed that the United States and the Soviet Union should agree on a list of devices that should not be tested in space.

As Karen Puschel observed, the Soviet leadership was exploring two possible solutions to the SDI dilemma: either an explicit agreement about the limits of what would be permitted or else simply a general agreement to adhere strictly to the ABM Treaty and deal with controversial issues on a case-by-case basis. Evidently it was not possible to obtain American agreement to the first of these options, and therefore Gorbachev settled for the latter at the Washington summit in December 1987 when the INF Treaty was signed. In the final analysis, the most Gorbachev got the Reagan administration to agree to was a commitment to adhere to the ABM Treaty for a specified period of time. A mark of the substantial shift in Soviet attitudes was Gorbachev's agreement to the proposal that if, after the non-withdrawal period, agreement on a strategic defence regime had not been reached, each side could decide for itself what to do about ballistic missile defence.

All the indications are that the shift in Soviet policy on SDI did not in itself mark a change in attitudes towards space-based ballistic missile defence. It seemed to be driven primarily by the need to make substantial progress in arms control. Given that for the time being – while Reagan was President – the United States had an unshakeable commitment to SDI, Gorbachev came to accept an agreement to postpone all the hard and dangerous questions for another day when the climate would be more propitious. There was also evidently a reassessment of the significance of SDI. As has been pointed out, by 1986 Soviet writings expressed greater scepticism as regards the feasibility of SDI, emphasizing its susceptibility to countermeasures. Clearly, the military-technical dangers emanating from SDI had been exaggerated, and Gorbachev had inadvertently given SDI a highly inflated bargaining value for the United States in arms control negotiations.[16] Furthermore, the difficulties faced by the programme in the United States made it appear possible that SDI would begin to fizzle out after Reagan left the presidency. Under President Bush, the programme has continued to receive a high level of funding, but expectations concerning its contribution to American security have been scaled down to the level of scientific reality, and SDI has therefore lost much of its political salience.

Conclusion

There are a number of conclusions to be drawn from this. The first is that contrary to some Western commentators' views, the Soviet participation in the ABM Treaty of 1972 did represent a genuine acceptance of the desirability of maintaining strict limits on strategic defence and of the stabilizing function of mutual vulnerability. This conclusion is not contradicted by continuing work on the Moscow ABM system and research in advanced technologies with possible applications for ballistic missile defence. There is not much prospect of a Soviet ballistic missile defence system that could seriously mitigate the effects of Western offensive strategic weapons even in post-START conditions. In terms of British interests, the 'Moscow criterion' is satisfied by the Chevaline system, which is already deployed, and the Trident D5 system which, when deployed in the configuration currently under discussion, will represent a serious increase in British strategic capabilities not justified by Soviet ABM modernization.

SDI's most important effect on East-West relations has been its role as a stumbling-block for arms control negotiations. It is most unlikely to have any effect on the Conventional Forces in Europe (CFE) talks which currently receive most of the public and official attention, nor will it hinder a START agreement. However, after the reductions envisaged in START, the unresolved issues of ballistic missile defence will resurface. At some point the Western alliance will be forced to take a serious look at its goals and objectives, and at arms control and the place of strategic defence in a future global security regime.

6
THEATRE NUCLEAR WEAPONS

In the late 1950s, despite the impressive Sputnik launch, the Soviet Union possessed only extremely limited means to attack the continental United States. The development of Soviet military power, in particular the capability to deliver nuclear strikes, was far more impressive in the European region. In 1955 the Soviet Union had 1,296 bombers for use in a regional theatre, 25 battlefield nuclear missiles and a total estimated stockpile of 324 warheads (which meant that a large number of the bombers would be used to deliver conventional bombs). By 1960, 200 land-based missiles of medium-range had been deployed (the SS-3 and SS-4), together with 50 short-range missiles and 36 medium-range missiles deployed on submarines. The Soviet Union under Khrushchev continued to build up its INF forces; in 1961, the SS-5 entered service, and by the time he was ousted there were 705 land-based missiles of medium range deployed, and 105 medium range sea-based missiles (some of which had the capability to strike the United States through forward deployment).[1]

It is clear, therefore, that in the 1950s the Soviet leadership made a decision to give priority to regional capabilities. They were maintained and built up even when in the 1960s large intercontinental strategic forces emerged.

The strategic thinking of the early 1950s was based on the lessons of World War II; nuclear weapons merely provided greater firepower. The build-up of regional power was thus dictated by military logic in the period before large-scale attacks on the continental

Theatre nuclear weapons

United States became possible. As the revolutionary effect of nuclear weapons on military affairs came to be recognized, the Soviet military began to adopt a policy of strategic pre-emption, but lacked the means to implement it at intercontinental range. Its sizeable regional force therefore served two strategic functions: one was to target the large number of American nuclear forces which were deployed in forward positions (particularly in Europe); the other was to deter an American attack on the Soviet Union by holding Western Europe hostage.

Soviet military doctrine at the time was based on the premise that any East-West war would involve the use of nuclear weapons from the outset (which was understandable in the context of the American doctrine of 'massive retaliation'). As a result Soviet intermediate-range nuclear forces had a very concrete military role, which remained even as their strategic deterrence function declined with the growth of the Soviet ICBM arsenal.

When the possibility that a war might remain at the non-nuclear level became an important element in Soviet military planning in the late 1960s, intermediate-range forces acquired new military and political functions. Whereas previously they were part of a strategy of pre-emption, they now had to be integrated in a process of escalation. The technological limitations of the existing intermediate-range ballistic missile (IRBM) force – the long time needed to prepare them for firing and their lack of accuracy, which made them unsuitable for counterforce strikes – made Soviet INF modernization imperative. Intermediate-range nuclear forces were also important in relation to China. A medium-term solution to this problem was achieved by designating part of the SS-11 force (the SS-11 was a variable range missile, the Soviet counterpart to the American Minuteman ICBM) to regional targets. By 1975, 350 SS-11s were deployed in this manner (120 in the Far East). Regional targets could of course also be covered by SLBMs; in 1975 there were 89 SS-N-4/N-5 and 480 SS-N-6 medium-range SLBMs (these figures do not include those which could reach US territory by virtue of forward deployment).[2]

These were clearly mere stop-gap measures. The next generation of Soviet long-range theatre nuclear forces emerged in the mid-1970s with the Tu-22M Backfire bomber and the SS-20 missile. The Backfire became operational in 1974 and was capable of nuclear and non-nuclear missions. Its range was just subcontinental, engender-

Theatre nuclear weapons

ing a controversy in the United States about whether or not it should be counted as a strategic system in SALT II. The SS-20 (Soviet designation RSD-10) was a MIRVed missile with three warheads and much greater accuracy than the existing LRTNFs. Deployment began in 1977.

The Soviet SS-20 programme played an important role in the controversy in the West that led to NATO's LRTNF modernization decision of 1979. In particular, German Chancellor Helmut Schmidt drew attention to the 'Eurostrategic imbalance' caused by the SS-20. The concern about Soviet LRTNF modernization was in stark contrast to previous attitudes to asymmetries in the European theatre. During the 1960s, despite the large number of Soviet medium-range missiles, the United States had withdrawn all its equivalent systems such as the Thor and Jupiter ballistic missiles and the Mace and Matador cruise missiles. From the West German point of view, the Multilateral Force project of the 1960s was designed to create a balancing medium-range force, but the United States believed that it was not needed for that reason. The interpretation of the Soviet motives and objectives which lay behind the SS-20 deployment lies at the heart of the debate about the meaning of the INF Treaty of 1987 when it was agreed that all the SS-20s would be withdrawn.

In the age of American strategic superiority, Soviet medium-range systems were interpreted as serving the function of deterring the United States by holding Europe hostage. The age of parity, as codified in SALT, implied, in the view of some European experts including Helmut Schmidt, the effective neutralization of the strategic forces of the superpowers. With extended deterrence in doubt, the 'Eurostrategic balance' acquired a new significance. Furthermore, American forward-based systems capable of reaching Soviet territory (such as the F-111 and F-4 bombers) could no longer be counted on to penetrate Soviet air defences. In this light, the SS-20 appeared to represent a qualitatively new capability, developed to undermine NATO's strategy of flexible response, to enable the USSR to engage in a limited nuclear war in Europe and thus to exert considerable political pressure on Western Europe towards neutralism and concessions to Soviet political objectives.

The history of the INF negotiations from 1981 to 1983 has been well documented elsewhere. Both political and military considerations must be taken into account when evaluating the Soviet negotiating strategy. Soviet analysis of the military threat focuses on perceived American endeavours to escape the realities of nuclear parity and recover military superiority and the capability to engage in military conflict either directly against the Soviet Union or, if deterred by Soviet military might, aimed at damaging other Soviet foreign policy interests (such as national liberation movements). Thus early Soviet comment on the NATO doctrine of 'flexible response' described it as a way of keeping nuclear war limited to Europe. Since then criticism of the Pentagon doctrine of 'limited war' has been a standard feature of Soviet attacks on American military policy. This was further developed in relation to Schlesinger's selective targeting doctrine:

> Schlesinger's announcement of the 'limited nuclear war concept' was another step in the development of counterforce aspects of US strategy. It reflected the obsession of US leaders with somehow breaking out of the restrictive situation of strategic nuclear parity between the USSR and the United States.[3]

The 'countervailing strategy' of the Carter administration and in particular Presidential Directive 59, which in the words of Trofimenko 'provided for a "limited counterforce war" against the Soviet Union',[4] was interpreted in a similar manner. This strategy, it was noted, was accompanied by disturbing new weapons systems with counterforce capabilities, including the MX missile, the Trident missile and cruise missiles; the Rapid Deployment Force also featured high among Soviet concerns. The rhetoric sharpened considerably during the first Reagan administration. The Republican Party's election programme endorsed the restoration of American strategic superiority. Reagan had promised a substantial rearmament programme. High-ranking representatives of the administration carelessly expounded the virtues of 'limited war', 'nuclear demonstration shots' and 'prevailing in a nuclear war'. The emerging American force posture began to look more and more threatening as East-West relations plunged to new depths, with President Reagan describing the Soviet Union as 'the focus of evil in the modern world'. The announcement of the Strategic Defence Initiative in March 1983 contributed to the view that the United States was seeking a first-strike capability.

In the context of these other developments, the planned deploy-

Theatre nuclear weapons

ment in Europe of cruise and Pershing II missiles took on a quite different significance. It was not just an addition to NATO's theatre forces, or even a counter to the SS-20. It was seen as providing the United States with a *completely new capability*. The villain of the piece was clearly the Pershing II, which could fit into a first-strike strategy as a system to attack the Soviet command-and-control centres. But even the slow-flying cruise missile was described as a first-strike weapon by Soviet commentators. *Krasnaya zvezda* stated: 'A new generation of cruise missiles could be supersonic and the flight time so reduced as to make a strike virtually a surprise attack.'[5]

It is difficult, of course, to disentangle the rhetoric from the underlying perception. How seriously did the Soviet leadership really take the threat posed by the NATO LRTNF deployments? Some Soviet specialists reportedly disagreed with the characterization of GLCMs as first-strike weapons. It is more likely that the Soviet Union was concerned that the threat of a Europe-based capability to penetrate its airspace, which was previously posed by forward-based aircraft but had been largely overcome by the improvements in Soviet air defences, was now being reintroduced with a vengeance. The Pershing II was clearly a more serious threat as part of a potential first strike; but even here Soviet perceptions differed. The argument concerned the range of the Pershing II, which according to official US statements is 1,000 nautical miles, allowing it to hit targets in the western Soviet Union from bases in West Germany. Some Soviet commentators claimed that the Pershing II had a range of 1,500 nautical miles, which would mean it could reach Moscow, but others accepted the official range.[6] None the less, it appears that there was genuine concern in the Soviet military that the Pershing II posed a new threat to command, control, communications and intelligence installations and theatre headquarters in the western Soviet Union. From the Soviet point of view, the planned LRTNF deployments were designed to enable the United States to conduct a limited nuclear war in Europe which would involve Soviet territory while leaving US territory intact.

The question thus arises: if the NATO modernization plans represented such a threat, and since as a result of the West's 'zero option' offer (to abandon modernization in exchange for withdrawal of all SS-20s) the Soviet Union could have forestalled deployment through arms control, why did the Soviet leadership not do so? As Western opponents of the zero option have since pointed out, the

Soviet Union could use other missiles to cover the targets assigned to the SS-20. Military considerations alone would perhaps have suggested such a course, although the military significance of the modernization is frequently exaggerated. From a political perspective, however, domestic dissent in the European NATO member states about security policy and the resulting tensions within the alliance appeared to serve Soviet policy interests even if ultimately they would prove unable to prevent deployment.

It must be added that the zero option itself constituted a very demanding form of arms control. Arms control until then had consisted largely either in banning things which no one intended to do anyway (or, as in the Partial Test Ban Treaty, ceasing a practice which was no longer necessary), or limiting deployment near existing or projected levels. Soviet arms control (as opposed to propagandistic disarmament schemes) resembled other Soviet foreign policy initiatives in that it was generally directed at maintaining the status quo. The idea of scrapping an already deployed new class of weapons (thus engaging in a form of retreat) was something else entirely. With the paralysis of leadership in the Soviet Union during the late Brezhnev/Andropov/Chernenko years it was apparently not possible to make the adaptations needed in order to take advantage of such unconventional opportunities.

With the arrival of Gorbachev many of the major assumptions of Soviet arms control became subject to fundamental revision. The INF negotiations provided a good example of the implications of the new political thinking. The threat of nuclear war was most acute in the European theatre, where the conventional forces of both blocs were so highly concentrated and where so much would be at stake in the event of an outbreak of hostilities. Moscow's adoption of a unilateral 'no first use' policy reflected the Soviet concern about the dangers of escalation and about tactical nuclear warfare. The denuclearization of Europe became an even more important objective under Gorbachev. The 'zero option' offer provided a good opportunity to demonstrate the new flexibility and dynamism of Soviet policy. As Gorbachev attempted to push the arms control process forward at various levels, it became clear that at the strategic level considerable obstacles remained. The firm commitment of the Reagan administration to SDI did not allow for rapid progress on a nuclear test ban or START, since the Soviet leadership was not willing to contemplate strategic arms reductions without some constraints on SDI. In any case, as it eventually turned out, the issues involved in START were rather complex. INF was therefore one area in which comparatively rapid progress could be made.

Three major issues had to be resolved before an INF agreement could be concluded: the extent of the reductions envisaged; the role of the British and French nuclear forces; and the relationship to SDI.

As part of the radical programme of nuclear disarmament announced in January 1986, Gorbachev embraced the 'zero option' at the European level. This meant eliminating all American and Soviet intermediate-range nuclear forces in the European theatre. The Americans, however, insisted that missiles in Asia must be included in any INF agreement. At the Reykjavik summit, it was agreed that an INF agreement should involve the removal of all US and Soviet intermediate-range nuclear forces from Europe and the limitation to 100 of INF warheads deployed in Asia. Although the Reykjavik package did not result in an agreement because of the linkage with SDI, it was greeted by European policy-makers with considerable, if publicly restrained, alarm, to the great surprise of both the Soviets and the Americans.

Just like the Strategic Defence Initiative in 1983, the Reykjavik proposals revealed that the Reagan administration and the Soviet leadership saw the role of nuclear weapons and arms control in a completely different light from the Europeans. From the European perspective, the purpose of arms control was not to eliminate nuclear weapons but to legitimize nuclear deterrence and provide it with a degree of stability. The Reykjavik proposals (involving deep cuts and eventual elimination of all ballistic missiles) threatened to undermine extended deterrence, while at the same time turning implementation of the 'zero option' into a realistic prospect. European reservations about the Reykjavik proposals, and their preference for an INF agreement which would allow the United States and the Soviet Union to retain 100 intermediate-range nuclear missiles in the European theatre, were expressed at the Nuclear Planning Group meeting two weeks after Reykjavik. When Federal Chancellor Helmut Kohl visited Washington, while publicly supporting President Reagan, he apparently expressed reservations about a zero INF agreement, claiming that it exposed Western Europe to Soviet shorter-range weapons.[7] When Paul Nitze visited Western Europe to explain US arms control policy to the allies, the

British also voiced misgivings about the zero option.[8] The effect of such alliance concerns was not to rule out the 'zero option', but rather to widen it, by increasing the pressure for the inclusion of short-range intermediate nuclear forces above 500 km. It had always been part of the American negotiating position to seek concurrent constraints on shorter-range systems alongside an INF agreement, but given the prolonged stalemate on INF this issue did not receive much attention until the Soviets deployed additional SRINF in Eastern Europe (about forty-eight modernized SS-12s) as a 'countermeasure' to US Pershing II and cruise missile deployments. Gorbachev's January 1986 offer relegated SRINF to a second reduction period in the 1990s; in February Shevardnadze added that the SRINF which had been deployed in response to American INF deployments would be withdrawn alongside US INF reductions.[9]

Under the influence of West German pressure, the Reagan Administration proposed a limitation of SRINF to either current Soviet or 1982 levels with reductions to be negotiated at a later stage. At Reykjavik, Gorbachev accepted the principle that limitations on SRINF should be laid down in an INF agreement. However, this was conceived in the form of a freeze at current levels (instead of a common ceiling), which would not allow the United States to compensate for its INF withdrawals by introducing new shorter-range systems, and thus was clearly unacceptable to the US. The American position at the Geneva negotiations remained for some time that there should be a global ceiling at present Soviet levels on missiles with ranges from 500 to 1,000 km and immediate negotiations for their reduction following an INF treaty. In the ensuing intra-alliance debate on the zero option, which was marked by uneasiness about the withdrawal of American INF on the one hand and reluctance to reject this opportunity for arms control on the other, SRINF became a dominant issue. This was recognized by Gorbachev when on 14 April 1987 he finally made an offer of an extended zero option to include SRINF in the 500 to 1,000 km range. Since NATO had no weapons in this category there could be no objection, and all obstacles to the successful conclusion of an INF treaty were finally removed when NATO agreed to include the Pershing IA missiles in the deal against the opposition of the West German government.

The INF agreement eventually signed is more far-reaching and numerically more advantageous to the West than all the various zero option proposals. The INF agreement radically distinguishes itself from previous arms control agreements by: (1) the extent of actual reductions (rather than limitations); (2) the extent of verification measures agreed; and (3) the large degree of asymmetry, which requires the Soviet Union to eliminate a much greater number of weapons deployed.

On the issue of the British and French systems Gorbachev also gradually gave substantial ground. As former Chief of the General Staff Akhromeev pointed out during the Supreme Soviet Presidium debates on the ratification of the INF treaty: 'The governments of both Great Britain and France categorically rejected the idea that these weapons should be a subject of the negotiations. We had, probably, to take into account the fact that they are independent states...' Shevardnadze stated even more openly in February 1988: 'the maintenance of deadlock at the talks on the English and French missile systems would have meant the absence of any accord at all'.[10]

The degree of Soviet flexibility on this issue can best be appreciated if we consider the original framework in which the British and French systems were discussed. In the first phase of the INF negotiations (1981–3) the central Soviet objective was to forestall American INF deployments entirely while maintaining the deployment of some SS-20s. The demand for the inclusion of British and French forces in the calculation of the Eurostrategic balance was not intended to bring about the scrapping of the British and French forces, but rather to buttress the Soviet arguments in favour of the legitimacy of their own deployments. Indeed, at one point the Soviets offered to reduce the number of their SS-20 warheads to the number of warheads deployed by Britain and France, thus making these countries' systems the sole legitimation for the SS-20 force. The acceptance of the zero option by the Gorbachev leadership, excluding the British and French forces from consideration, constituted therefore a major shift in the Soviet negotiating position. By January 1986 Gorbachev had already conceded the point that the British and French systems would not be counted in the INF accord. He still sought to link INF to a freeze on the British and French systems, but he subsequently dropped even this precondition.

As far as linkage with SDI is concerned, Soviet policy underwent curious reversals. In October 1985 Gorbachev had agreed to negotiate on INF separately, without any conditions involving SDI. At the Reykjavik summit the linkage had been re-established but, as we have seen in the previous chapter, it was subsequently removed to allow the successful negotiation of the treaty. These shifts had less to do with the issue of INF and more with the evolution of Soviet objectives with regard to SDI. As the restraint of SDI became less important, greater flexibility ensued.

European security after the INF agreement

A close analysis of Soviet behaviour in arms control since the advent of Gorbachev, particularly in the area of INF, shows it to be somewhat less innovative and imaginative than it might at first appear. In effect, as NATO insisted on its conditions for the success of the INF negotiations, Gorbachev continually gave ground until an acceptable settlement was reached. Although Gorbachev met all Western demands, the INF agreement has subsequently been criticized in the West.

The critics, such as West German arms control expert Jürgen Todenhöfer, have argued that the agreement is in Soviet, not in Western interests.[11] Some of the main arguments are:

(a) The deployment of LRTNF is necessary for the proper implementation of the strategy of flexible response and to prevent strategic decoupling. (American aircraft currently based in Europe are no longer considered adequate for this task.) The West German defence expert Uwe Nerlich stated bluntly that NATO should not accept an agreement resulting in the removal of US LRTNF from Europe, no matter what concessions the Soviets were prepared to make.[12] Indeed, the desire to have nuclear weapons systems based in Europe which can reach targets in the Soviet Union has been a long-standing feature of West German security policy, dating back to the time of Adenauer in the late 1950s. Thus, prior to the conclusion of the INF agreement, this author was told in the German Ministry of Defence that 'the zero option is the worst thing that could happen to us'. The pressure on the West German leadership to agree to the removal of the Pershing IA missiles, which on technical grounds (they were German, with American warheads) might have been considered exempt from the INF treaty, resulted in feelings of betrayal.

(b) The INF agreement starts arms reduction at the wrong end. For West Germany, the most problematic weapons systems are short-range theatre nuclear forces, since they are likely to be detonated on German territory, East or West. In the words of CDU party caucus chairman Alfred Dregger, 'The shorter the range the more German the effect' of using nuclear weapons.

(c) Since the Soviets have tested their variable-range ICBMs and can cover all the targets of SS-20s with other systems, the INF agreement does not result in any tangible reduction in the threat facing Western Europe.

(d) It has long been recognized by students of Soviet military doctrine that a shift from a nuclear emphasis to a conventional emphasis has occurred. It is now generally agreed among Western experts that in the event of war in Europe the Soviet Union would endeavour to keep hostilities below the nuclear threshold for as long as possible, given the risks that nuclear escalation would pose for the Soviet homeland. The denuclearization of Europe would therefore fit in well with the present requirements of Soviet military strategy, while reducing deterrence against Soviet aggression on the conventional level.[13]

Some of these arguments reflect the confusion in the official rationales for deploying NATO LRTNF in the first place. It has never been in doubt that the theatre could be targeted by central strategic systems from the Soviet Union or the United States. It was the deployment of a system of regional range (the SS-20) which was portrayed as a particular threat that needed to be countered. Whether NATO LRTNF are needed for strategic coupling and for the proper implementation of flexible response is a moot question. There is no solution for the problem of extended deterrence, since keeping conflict away from the continental United States will always be a priority for the Americans; nuclear weapons deployed in Europe can be considered as a means of keeping conflict limited to Europe. Nevertheless, the uncertainty associated with the presence of nuclear weapons has been sufficient to make war in Europe an unacceptable option for everyone. The Chernobyl incident has shown the Soviet leadership in particular the potentially disastrous consequences of even a low-level conflict involving only a few nuclear weapons, or even a conventional conflict in which nuclear power stations become targets. There is no reason to assume that any of the technical or political solutions for the problems of extended deterrence have had much influence on this basic reality. It is true that from the point of view of stable deterrence in Europe, the INF agreement starts arms control at the wrong end. Nevertheless, it does have important strategic features which enhance security in Europe.

One very important aspect of the implications for West German security policy of the double-zero agreement has been strangely ignored in most of the discussions about the costs and benefits of the INF treaty. During the debate about SDI, Defence Minister Manfred Wörner raised the issue of ATBMs (anti-tactical ballistic missile systems). The need for ATBMs was explained by reference to the improvement and diversification of Soviet nuclear-capable theatre ballistic missiles. Especially noted was the improvement in the accuracy of the SS-21, SS-22 and SS-23. In the view of Uwe Nerlich, if this trend continued, it could mean that 'missiles could thus eventually be substituted for aircraft in critical operations during the initial phase of an independent air operation, particularly in air defense suppression.'[14] It was noted that the Soviet Union apparently intended to arm some of its missiles with chemical and conventional warheads. Another important characteristic of these missiles is their mobility. However, with the zero option, this threat has been virtually removed. (Among the medium-range missiles to be removed under the INF agreement are the SS-12 and SS-23. The most important short-range missile still to remain is the SS-21, with a range of 150 km.) The demand for ATBMs has therefore faded away. For this reason alone, from the West German standpoint, the INF agreement must be considered a major enhancement of security, but this point has not really been emphasized in the post-INF debate.

Furthermore, an INF agreement was available. It is difficult to argue convincingly that war has in any sense become more likely because of the INF agreement. If it becomes part of a transition to a more stable military situation in Europe, then there is no question that it has made a substantial contribution to Western security.

Short-range nuclear forces: towards a third zero?
The debate on short-range nuclear force modernization within NATO has also proved very divisive and could have become as serious as the INF controversy. Once again, West Germany has been at the centre. The INF arguments brought about a decisive

shift in public attitudes, increasing opposition to a nuclear defence policy: this has had a permanent effect that no politician can ignore. One of the surprising features of the current debate is that pressure to move towards a 'third zero' – i.e. elimination by both sides of battlefield nuclear weapons – is coming not merely from the Social Democrats and the Greens, but even from within the conservative CDU/CSU. None other than the president of the party caucus, Alfred Dregger, has advanced the notion that West Germany is 'singularized' on the grounds that most of the theatre nuclear weapons are now based there, thus making it a unique target for Soviet attack; furthermore in case of conflict these weapons would be detonated on German soil (East or West). This debate was given additional impetus by a report on 'Discriminate Deterrence' commissioned by the US government and written by Fred Iklé and Alfred Wohlstetter. The report emphasized the military ('warfighting') function of theatre nuclear weapons and explicitly argued against assigning them the function of 'coupling' to the US strategic arsenal, thus denying a central tenet of NATO nuclear doctrine and causing considerable alarm, especially among the conservatives in Germany, despite the unofficial nature of the document.[15]

The most controversial aspect of SNF modernization is currently the question of nuclear missiles and artillery. The emphasis given to the issue of the Lance missiles, which will become obsolete in the mid-1990s, has obscured a much more fundamental problem.[16] During the recent Wintex-Cimex exercises, in which implementation of the NATO 'General Political Guidelines for the Initial Use of Tactical Nuclear Weapons' was practised, three nuclear weapons were hypothetically detonated in East Germany, one in the Soviet Union, one in Turkey and more in other parts of Eastern Europe. The results of this war game confirmed German fears that they would be the victims of any nuclear conflict in Europe. Furthermore, they indicated that in the event of a Soviet attack West Germany might be unwilling to implement NATO strategy. Former Chancellor Helmut Schmidt took the view that as soon as the first nuclear weapon was about to be released, he would order the complete cessation of all hostilities. This fundamental ambivalence towards the NATO strategy of flexible response is of much greater significance than the debates about SNF modernization.

As in the INF debate, the military and political rationales for nuclear artillery modernization are confused. The plain fact is that there is no military necessity for nuclear artillery in Central Europe. Any conceivable military mission can be accomplished by other means, such as aircraft based in Europe, or submarine-based missiles. Indeed, nuclear artillery can have a negative effect in military terms in two ways. The strategy of flexible response envisages keeping any conflict in Central Europe at the conventional level for as long as possible. The need to protect vulnerable land-based nuclear weapons against conventional enemy attack would result in a substantial diversion of resources and thus would make it more difficult to keep the nuclear threshold high; even worse, the imminent loss of the land-based nuclear weapons might encourage their use. On another level, NATO SNF modernization could encourage the modernization of Soviet short-range missiles. What German military planners fear in particular is the conversion of nuclear short-range missiles for conventional use, enabling a general attack on a wide range of military targets deep inside NATO territory without the use of nuclear weapons.

Deterrence in Europe is very stable, with or without SNF modernization. As Denis Healey has pointed out, it takes 5% of deterrence to deter the Soviets, but 95% to reassure the allies.[17] The only contribution nuclear artillery could make to Western security lies in its political symbolism as a reassurance to allies, in particular to the West Germans. The problem is, however, that it does not reassure. On the contrary, many West Germans feel more threatened by the presence of American nuclear weapons than by the Soviet Union.

There has been pressure from the Soviet Union for a move towards a 'third zero'. On 11 May 1989 Gorbachev announced the unilateral withdrawal of 500 short-range nuclear weapons: 284 missile warheads, 166 aircraft-delivered weapons and 50 artillery-delivered weapons. An official Tass statement noted that the Soviet Union would withdraw all nuclear ammunition from the territory of the WTO countries in 1989–91 if NATO reciprocated.[18]

This has significant implications for arms control. It is important that SNF modernization should not be perceived as a circumvention of the INF treaty. This would be the case if weapons were introduced, particularly stand-off missiles on aircraft, which could reach Soviet territory. The Soviets were particularly concerned that the Lance modernization issue might be used as a political diversion to cover the introduction of air-launched missiles. Another important issue for arms control is that the proposed successor system for Lance is to be based on the Multiple Launch Rocket System (MLRS), thus making it a nuclear-capable system. This will introduce complications into arms control that may prove horrendously difficult to resolve. A Western proposal to eliminate all nuclear artillery with a range above 125 km would have a number of significant military and political benefits. It would eliminate an important category of threatening weapons from the Soviet arsenal and forestall their modernization. It would restore the trust of Western populations in the security policy of their governments by demonstrating a constructive attitude and it would allow NATO to regain some initiative on the arms control agenda. It would also avoid a possibly divisive debate in the alliance.

There are some signs that the Soviet leadership is backing away from playing West European politics with the SNF modernization issue. Among Soviet specialists, the realization has come that in conditions of radical conventional arms reductions the presence of some nuclear weapons in Europe may contribute to stability.[19] Soviet acceptance of TNF in Europe will depend to some extent on the types of weapons involved: air-launched weapons that can reach Soviet territory will almost certainly be rejected as 'offensive'. The SNF modernization issue can be shelved until the first phase of CFE has been agreed, but it is imperative that in the meantime an agreed framework for proceeding on this issue should be worked out within the alliance and the Soviet Union.

7
CONVENTIONAL FORCE PLANNING

We have already indicated the position of 'reasonable sufficiency' in the framework of military doctrine. The question which has received most attention in the West is how this concept is to be put into practice, what the implications are for the restructuring of the Soviet armed forces and for arms control. The first issue, which is a rather sensitive one, is whether the concept of sufficiency implies that changes in the level of Soviet forces are necessary. The Soviet view of the sources of tension in East-West relations has always been that it arises from the fundamental contradictions between capitalism and socialism. Thus there is a conflict at the systemic level, but the response of the Soviet Union to this in the postwar era has been to promote a state of peaceful coexistence. Capitalist states, on the other hand, were seen as being driven by imperialism and thus actively promoting conflict with socialism and among themselves. Thus the blame for the Cold War and the arms race was firmly put at the door of the United States and its allies. The engine of the arms race was the military-industrial complex of the advanced capitalist states. Implicit in this analysis was the view that such forces did not operate in the Soviet Union, which was merely safeguarding the gains of socialism against external threats; Soviet military forces therefore were kept at a level sufficient for this task. In this sense, the concepts of sufficiency and a defensive force posture have been implicit in the official Soviet position for quite some time. In 1982 Leonid Brezhnev stated about Soviet defence expenditure: 'We have

Conventional force planning

not spent, nor will we spend, a single rouble more for these purposes than is absolutely necessary for assuring the security of our people.'[1]

The development of the concept of 'reasonable sufficiency' by civilian academics and its adoption by the Gorbachev leadership poses a direct challenge to this interpretation and to the interests of the military establishment in general, which was well served by the old interpretation of sufficiency. The vagueness of the concept of reasonable sufficiency is therefore deliberate to some extent. It is, as Stephen Meyer has put it, a 'political wildcard'[2] which can be used both in foreign relations and the domestic institutional battles with the advocates of higher military spending. One fundamental issue which has not been clarified in the Soviet debate so far is the extent to which a sufficient level of military forces is defined by the external military environment. At one end of the spectrum of views on this issue, reasonable sufficiency means that one simply matches the forces of the opponent and does not increase one's military potential any further. This would, however, lock the Soviet Union into precisely the kind of action-reaction dynamic that the new thinking is designed to get it out of. In this context, Soviet scholars have drawn attention to what they describe as the 'Competition Strategy' concept:

> Drawing on the established differences in the economic positions of the two sides and in a bid to do all in its power to increase the burden of the arms race for the USSR with specially oriented military programmes, the West is striving in the foreseeable future to put the Soviet Union before a quite definite dilemma – either reconcile itself to military superiority of the USA and its allies (including formalisation thereof in inequitable arms limitation agreements) or face economic upheavals under the onus of increasingly costly military competition.[3]

Asymmetric responses are advocated as a means of neutralizing the 'Competition Strategy'. As an example, Zhurkin, Karaganov and Kortunov cite the asymmetric response by the Soviet Union to the American strategic bomber threat in the late 1950s, when the Khrushchev leadership proceeded with the development of ICBMs instead of strategic bombers.[4] Another obvious example is the decision to respond to a full-blown SDI programme – should it ever

81

come to fruition – not by a Soviet version, but by the build-up of offensive forces to saturate the defence.

There is, however, scope for further development of the notion of 'reasonable sufficiency', since sufficiency can also be understood as a principle for the unilateral restructuring of Soviet forces. This is easily understandable at the strategic nuclear level where 'minimum deterrence' is a long-established concept. But even at the conventional level, unilateral restructuring and force reductions have been advocated. That there is some scope for unilateral actions has been accepted by the political leadership, as demonstrated by the unilateral reductions announced by Gorbachev at the United Nations in December 1988 against the views of the military leadership (in particular Akhromeev).

Shortly after the Warsaw Pact declaration on military doctrine in May 1987, Minister of Defence Yazov put forward a definition of nuclear and conventional sufficiency which was clearly at odds with the more far-reaching ideas proposed by the civilian analysts. It highlights very clearly the two different sides of the debate.

> When we speak of maintaining the armed forces and their military potential at levels of reasonable sufficiency, we have in mind that at the present stage the essence of sufficiency for the strategic forces of the Soviet Union is determined by the necessity of not permitting a nuclear attack without retribution under any, even the most unfavourable circumstances. For conventional means, sufficiency involves a quantity and quality of armed forces and arms capable of reliably assuring the collective defence of the socialist community. The limits of reasonable sufficiency are set not by us, but by the actions of the United States and NATO. The countries of the Warsaw Pact do not seek military superiority or aspire to greater security, but they will not accept less security or permit military superiority over themselves.[5]

Similar statements were made by the former Chief of the General Staff S. Akhromeev.[6]

It must be said that Gorbachev himself at the 27th Party Congress in 1986 implied that the level of sufficiency for Soviet armed forces would depend on the West. An editorial in the General Staff journal *Voennaya mysl'* in January 1988 expounded the view that defence sufficiency could not be unilateral; it could only be understood on the principle of military equivalence, and the extent to which the Soviet Union could move towards a posture of sufficiency was limited by the actions of the USA and NATO.[7] The formulation of the new Warsaw Pact military doctrine in May 1987 left the military free to interpret the requirements of a sufficient and 'reliable' defence as implying maintenance of the existing military balance. An editorial published in the journal *Zarubezhnoe voennoe obozrenie* is a good example of how official military statements pay lip-service to the new doctrine, but an analysis of the use of terms such as 'reliable defence at the level of sufficiency' shows that they really belong to the old thinking.[8] The requirements of sufficiency could be and have been taken to imply that Warsaw Pact forces are already at a level of sufficiency.

The critical issue which divides military representatives from civilian analysts is the link between sufficiency and parity. For the civilian analysts, the concept of 'parity' embodies the failure of arms control to halt the arms race, whereas for the military leaders it represents the crucial conceptual device in their rearguard action to maintain conventional forces at present levels, since it has been argued (at least until recently) that a rough parity currently exists between Warsaw Pact and NATO forces. Thus Army General Anatoly Gribkov and Admiral Kostev have supported the principle of reasonable sufficiency in defence, but referred to parity as a measure of sufficiency.[9] Similarly Marshal Viktor G. Kulikov, former Chief of the General Staff, stressed the relationship between parity and sufficiency. He also made it clear that while asymmetries existed between the NATO and WTO force postures, the overall balance of forces was characterized by parity, which needed to be preserved in arms reductions.[10] Kulikov seems to exhibit some measure of agreement with the civilian analysts in so far as he considers parity at a high level to be dangerous, since in such a situation it is more difficult to cope with a surprise attack. The concept of defence sufficiency serves as an instrument for developing a 'rational attitude' towards ending the arms race and proceeding with disarmament. Army General Ivan Tret'yak, Commander-in-Chief of the Air Defence Forces (PVO), has been a particularly outspoken opponent of force reductions, using the experience of the unilateral troop reductions during the Khrushchev period as a negative example.[11] Lieutenant General Vladimir Serebryannikov, who has published some of the more outspoken and analytically substantive critiques of the new thinking in military affairs, has warned of discrepancies between political and military means to secure peace. He has stated that 'reasonable sufficiency is clearly interrelated to military-strategic parity'.[12]

According to Serebryannikov's analysis, the postwar era has been characterized by the transition from a situation where the military means of guaranteeing security were predominant over the political means to the present situation where the political means are decisive. The reason for this is to be found both in the existence of large nuclear arsenals which have made it impossible to resolve international disputes by means of war and the general global interdependence which acts as a constraint on the aggressiveness of imperialism. However, political means are only effective under two conditions: (i) the abandonment of the old thinking – i.e. the striving for military superiority; (ii) the maintenance of a strategic military balance, which requires of the Soviet Union a high combat-readiness. Soviet military power serves to strengthen the political means of security and permits the transfer of the historical competition between imperialism and socialism away from the military to the peaceful arena.[13]

Although opposition to unilateral force reductions was the principal theme of military statements on this issue prior to the reductions announced by Gorbachev at the UN General Assembly in December 1988, it is known that other views also exist in the Soviet military. The effectiveness of Soviet army units in terms of equipment, discipline and combat readiness varies considerably. To cut down the 'dead wood' and concentrate resources on creating a smaller but more effective Soviet army could therefore result in a considerable enhancement of military fighting capabilities.[14] Similar arguments have been used by civilian analysts to support the notion of a professional army of 1.5–2 million men and the abolition of military service. Such proposals are still rejected out of hand by the military leadership.

It is evident that the link between parity and sufficiency is undeniable unless one finds a new set of criteria to define the needs of national defence which differs from the traditional Soviet one. Much of the work of the civilian analysts has been directed towards this end. They have questioned military assumptions with regard to threat assessment, the kind of war the Soviet Union should be prepared to fight, and the strategy which should define Soviet defence preparations.

The military assessment depicts the United States and NATO as intent on attacking and dominating the socialist camp. The military doctrine of the United States and NATO is interpreted as offensive; NATO military capabilities and force deployments are viewed as evidence of aggressive intent. In the nuclear sphere, deployment of forward-based systems and concepts of 'limited war' are cited as evidence; as for conventional forces, the American airland battle concept and the NATO concept of follow-on-forces attack (FOFA) (designed to carry the battle forward into Warsaw Pact territory) are said to reveal the true nature of the West's intentions. Recent Soviet military analysis accepts the notion that superiority by the factor of 3 to 4 necessary for a successful offence cannot be created in secret prior to the initiation of war. However, Soviet military writers maintain that a surprise attack is still possible because of the enhanced firepower provided by new technologies. The threat of a surprise attack appears to be a constant theme running through Soviet military threat perceptions.[15] The term 'social revenge' has been used to describe the Western objective of destroying communism.[16] In 1987 Defence Minister Yazov spoke of the 'serious reality' of possible Western aggression against the socialist countries, while Chief of the General Staff Akhromeev likewise emphasized the constant military threat posed by imperialism.[17]

A challenge by Zhurkin, Karaganov and Kortunov to the military assessment of the threat facing the Soviet Union was contained in an article published in *Kommunist* in 1988. They asserted that the possibility of war in Europe on a conventional or nuclear level was virtually nil and that there was practically no reason to expect an invasion from the West, given the nature of Western democracies and the achievement of military parity at the strategic and theatre levels. They questioned the main threat scenario which forms the basis for Soviet military planning, which they see as based on a World War II vision of the world. Indeed, the German invasion of June 1941, they claimed, still lies at the basis of the threat perceptions of military leaders and the general public in the Soviet Union.

In the view of the academics, a new, accurate analysis of the international security environment in which the Soviet Union finds itself is necessary. One of their principal conclusions is that as a military confrontation in Central Europe is unlikely under the prevailing circumstances, the West has shifted the competition with the socialist system to the economic sphere. It is there that the main challenges which the Soviet Union faces to its security are to be found. Different criteria are therefore required for force planning. The economic advantage gained by reducing expenditure on the armed forces can make a significant contribution to the enhancement of national security.

As many in the West have argued, one of the principal reasons for the low probability of war in Central Europe is the existence of parity at the strategic nuclear level and the risks associated with any form of nuclear war. This is difficult to reconcile with the enthusiasm for denuclearization manifest in some Soviet writings and public statements. Aleksei Arbatov has frankly acknowledged the role of nuclear forces in reducing the likelihood of war:

> The enormous quantitative levels and the destructive force of conventional arms and armed forces and their saturation with tactical nuclear ammunition make extremely unlikely a lengthy wide-scale conventional war between the major military-political alliances in Europe or the Far East without it rapidly escalating into a wide-scale nuclear exchange.[18]

In Arbatov's view, then, the risk of escalation to the strategic level makes a large-scale war unlikely. He goes further to state that deterrence at the strategic nuclear level enables greater reductions at the theatre nuclear and conventional levels:

> ... the preservation of reliable deterrence at the highest and most important military level (strategic nuclear) means that less stringent requirements are acceptable for the security of the USSR and its allies at the lower, theatre nuclear and conventional forces levels. ... This provides an opportunity for substantially reducing in Europe the Warsaw Treaty Organization and NATO force levels, and rearranging force structures (that is, the complement of offensive and defensive arms) and deployment.[19]

It is clear that not all civilian analysts share Arbatov's views, and Zhurkin, Karaganov and Kortunov in particular have argued for complete denuclearization. However, no attempt has been made at a threat assessment assuming present levels of conventional forces and an absence of nuclear weapons, and it must be supposed that denuclearization will occur in conjunction with a movement towards 'reasonable sufficiency' in conventional terms.

Nevertheless, a different threat assessment alone is not enough to provide a rationale for the kind of restructuring and force reductions which the civilian analysts envisage. They also propose a different conception of the kind of war the Soviet Union would fight if it became subject to aggression. This is already implicit in the definition of reasonable sufficiency given by Zhurkin and his co-authors as a level of force sufficient to defend against aggression but insufficient to mount an aggressive blitzkrieg and take over the opponent's territory. In seeking to develop a new set of strategic concepts which allow the development of criteria for a Soviet force posture at much reduced levels, the civilian analysts have adopted ideas first elaborated by West German analysts about 'defensive defence'; that is, strategies and force postures which are capable of providing adequate defence but do not threaten others. As we have already pointed out, the adoption of a 'defensive strategy' and 'defensive objectives' has become an integral part of Soviet military doctrine. Nevertheless there is a wide range of interpretations of what that implies. In order to evaluate the possible implications of the new political thinking for military force postures, it is imperative to look in more detail at Soviet thinking about defensive defence.

Sufficiency and the strategy of defence

Soviet military doctrine has always claimed to be defensive in character. Soviet statements about the outbreak of war with the West have always assumed that aggression would come from the West, and that only if the Soviet Union were unable to deter the aggressors would it be necessary to rebuff them decisively. Likewise, large-scale military exercises have always been based on a scenario involving an attack by NATO forces. This defensive doctrine, however, was based on an offensive military strategy: in Soviet scenarios the result of a Western attack on Warsaw Pact territory was always the occupation of the adversary's territory by Warsaw Pact forces in theatres of conflict adjacent to Warsaw Pact territory.

Some critics have drawn attention to complications caused by the dichotomy between the defensiveness of Soviet military doctrine at the political level and the offensive strategies espoused at the military-technical level. Viktor Kulikov, for example, has argued that the defensive character of Soviet military doctrine did not find application in all aspects of its military-technical side.[20] Some Soviet commentators have taken the view that the offensive character of the military-technical side of Soviet military doctrine is essentially the result of Stalin's influence and a deviation from Leninist principles, a line of argument which conforms well with Gorbachev's justification of the new thinking as a return to true Leninist principles.[21]

The resulting debate about the nature of a defensive military strategy and the extent to which a 'defensive defence' is feasible has brought together two distinct strands in the evolution of Soviet military thought. In the late 1970s and early 1980s the Soviet military had taken a renewed interest in defensive operations for purely military reasons. The main catalyst in the re-evaluation of the role of defensive operations was the emergence of new technologies and the formulation of deep-strike operational concepts in the US airland battle and the NATO FOFA doctrines. It became evident that future deep-strike precision-guided weapons which could penetrate far into Warsaw Pact territory, destroying not merely the first echelon forces, but striking also against the second echelon and reserves, could enable a defender successfully to pre-empt preparations for the offensive. It might therefore not be possible to carry the offensive to the enemy's territory. There was a realization that the Soviet Union might not have sufficient early warning of a NATO attack to mobilize and engage in an offensive now that the new technologies had improved surprise attack capabilities. Thus Gareev envisages

> a war against the socialist states on a surprise attack, without the preliminary deployment of all the resources required for this ... early strategic deployment of the Armed Forces prior to the start of a war, regardless of all the benefits of this in purely military terms, is not always feasible out of military-political considerations ... the present system of strategic deployment cannot be oriented solely on one of the most advantageous variations for us, but should be more flexible and provide the organized deployment of the troops (forces) under any conditions when the imperialist aggressors initiate a war.[22]

Furthermore, the fact that the adversaries will be able to mount attacks deep inside each other's territories from the moment of the onset of hostilities implies that the theatre of war is considerably extended, thus making defensive operations an indispensable part of the war effort. These considerations prompted a whole series of military writings devoted to the study of defensive operations.[23] Gareev has succinctly summarized Soviet military thinking on the relation between strategic offence and defence:

> In speaking about the problems of offensive and defensive operations, it must be considered that at present there is an ever-stronger tendency toward a further merging of the methods of troop operations on the offensive and defensive. A modern offensive is a combination of fire strikes, the rapid advance of tanks and armoured infantry supported by aviation and helicopter gunships from the air and bold actions of airborne troops deep in the defenses and on the flanks of the opposing groupings. In contrast to an offensive in the period of the Great Patriotic War, this will be not a successive advance of the troops from line to line but a more decisive simultaneous hitting of the enemy to the entire depth of its configuration.[24]

Stephen Meyer has pointed to the reorganization of the air defences between 1978 and 1985 as a concrete measure 'intended to improve the integration of strategic and tactical air defense capabilities in general, and the defensive capabilities of Soviet ground forces in particular'.[25]

It is important to note that this emphasis on defensive operations in Soviet military thought is completely unrelated to the civilian notions of a non-provocative defence. It is quite clear from the various sources cited, and Gareev's book in particular, that defensive operations are not a substitute for but rather part and parcel of large-scale offensive operations. Defensive operations may be of particular significance during the initial period of war, and as a means to contain NATO counterstrikes. The inclusion of deep-strike capabilities as part of the defensive effort indicates that the defensive operations themselves involve offensive actions. Gareev himself emphasizes the convergence of 'offensive' and 'defensive' concepts.

The work by Soviet civilian experts on 'defensive defence' posits as the main objective of a defensive posture the reduction of the military potentials of each nation to the point where they retain only the capability to deny potential adversaries the means to invade and occupy their territory. This involves limitations on the general scope of warfare a country prepares to engage in, limitations on the kinds and numbers of armaments deployed, and new strategic and operational concepts that would make 'reasonable sufficiency' work. For one thing, as Zhurkin, Karaganov and Kortunov state, the notion of autonomous regional balances and the deployment of forces capable of achieving victory in several independent regional conflicts should be rejected, together with the idea of deploying forces equal to the total forces of all potential adversaries.[26]

The implementation of this principle would have a considerable effect on Soviet troop levels. Tactical nuclear weapons in particular have been considered part of an offensive weapons potential. But there is a long list of conventional weapons which would have no place in a defensive force posture and which are considered by Soviet civilian specialists to be particularly destabilizing. Andrei Kokoshin cites long-range precision-guided weapons, strike aviation, tanks, combat helicopters, long-range artillery and ballistic missiles as weapons which are designed for offensive operations.[27] Oleg Amirov, Nikolai Kishilov, Vadim Makarevsky and Yuri Usachev proposed that

> to implement the concept of 'non-offensive defense', along with reducing the overall level of military confrontation, it is necessary to give priority to the reduction of armaments with more clearly pronounced offensive functions: tanks, long-range artillery, tactical strike aircraft, tactical missiles, combat helicopters, and pontoon bridge facilities. More important than purely quantitative cuts is a restructuring of armed forces as reductions take place: disbanding some major armoured and mechanized forces together with their logistics support units, air armies and missile groups, and redeploying others to areas farther removed from the forward edge so that they could perform the function of an operational reserve for the defense, and not that of an attack to mount a surprise offensive.[28]

The most radical version of 'defensive defence', which has been proposed by A. A. Kokoshin and General V. Larionov, would completely renounce offensive or counteroffensive operations, and dismantle both sides' capacity for undertaking large-scale strategic offensives, by removing the types of armaments listed above.[29] Kokoshin and Kortunov also seem to have accepted the notion developed in West Germany of defence based on a territorial principle, and cite the example of neutral states in Europe which have developed significant defence capabilities without being able to mount large offensive operations.[30] A pioneering article on the role of defensive operations was the work by Kokoshin and Larionov which on the basis of an analysis of the battle of Kursk sought to demonstrate the value of defensive operations and thus directly engage with the arguments of the professional military.[31] The contrary argument was made by the Chief of the Ground Forces, General Ivanovsky, in an analysis of the battle of Stalingrad which emphasized defensive operations but maintained that the ultimate success of Soviet forces was due to counteroffensive operations.[32]

The first point which military spokesmen make in response to civilian 'defensive' theorists is that the Soviet Union already has a defensive force posture. Gareev, for example, has described the force levels of NATO and the WTO as roughly equal and stressed certain NATO advantages such as reserves and weapons production capacity to show that the WTO force deployments are not unreasonable. The defensive nature of Soviet military planning is always said to be rooted in the peace-loving nature of the Soviet state. Gareev was involved in directing much of the study done in the General Staff on defensive strategies. He and Minister of Defence Yazov maintain that the WTO already has a defensive strategy. Military leaders insist that it is not possible to repel a large-scale enemy attack successfully without shifting to the counteroffensive.

It must be pointed out, however, that the lines of the debate are not as clearly drawn as the above description may suggest. Most civilian analysts do accept the need for some level of counteroffensive. Aleksei Arbatov has made the point often heard in the West:

> The complexity of the problem of restructuring military strategy, operational plans and the levels, composition and technical equipment of the armed forces along defensive principles consists primarily in the fact that it is extremely difficult to divide combat equipment and armaments, and military units and forces into offensive and defensive categories.

Modern armed forces are very complex organizational-technical mechanisms founded on the interaction of a large number of separate elements which are characterized overall by high fire power and mobility. Moreover, *the same elements can perform either offensive or defensive operations depending on the combat mission* ... Another problem is that however strong the defense may be, an aggressor, by concentrating forces in one sector and resorting to a surprise attack and free manoeuvring, will in any case have a good chance of breaking through and advancing deep into the territory of the other side. *What is needed to repulse this kind of aggression is a huge counteroffensive potential* which, from an operational-tactical point of view, would carry out offensive tasks, and from the strategic-political view, defensive tasks.[33] [Emphasis added]

The debate thus revolves around the nature and extent of such a counteroffensive – its timing and objectives – and the force posture necessary to be able to implement it. Military writers still see the decisive defeat of NATO as the necessary objective, which would require the capability to occupy NATO territory as before. Aleksei Arbatov has stressed that the counteroffensive potential must not appear threatening to others and has expounded the view that the counteroffensive should be limited to the restoration of the status quo, on the basis that escalation to the nuclear level would become inevitable if the conflict was carried to the adversary's territory. Vitaly Shlykov's analysis of tank asymmetry demonstrates how Warsaw Pact capabilities many appear unduly threatening to the other side. A consequence, he writes, is that the tank asymmetry has been used as a 'catalyst of the arms race' by those in the West who oppose disarmament. This has helped to create the problem of a high level of tank confrontation in Europe.[34] An intermediate position has been advocated by General Lieutenant V. Serebryannikov of the Main Political Administration: the counteroffensive should halt after the enemy has been expelled and a negotiated end to the war should be attempted. If the enemy regroups his forces and prepares to launch another attack, the counteroffensive should move onto the adversary's territory.[35] Nevertheless, although few civilian analysts seem to be advocating a pure 'defensive defence', their strong emphasis on reductions and the restructuring of the Soviet

Conventional force planning

force posture on a partly unilateral, partly negotiated basis clearly provokes resistance in professional military quarters.

Political responses and compromises
The key issue is the attitude taken by the political leadership. As we have seen in Chapter 1, Gorbachev has identified himself quite explicitly with the concept of 'reasonable sufficiency', the notion of force reductions to a level of sufficiency, and asymmetric conventional force reductions. The professional military and the civilian analysts have both staked out positions that can just be accommodated within the language used by Gorbachev. There is no doubt that Gorbachev himself is the chief promoter of the new thinking and that his domestic political priorities are linked with radical changes in the international environment. The natural concomitant of the objective of a substantial reorientation of the economy away from the huge military apparatus is a changing strategic context that permits this to happen. Nevertheless, Gorbachev has been constrained by the institutional power of the military, and in terms of the formulation of military strategy and operational plans the professional military is still the dominant reservoir of expertise.[36] Thus, while the political discourse changed dramatically, no radical restructuring of Soviet forces occurred, engendering a deep scepticism in the West about the reality of the 'new thinking'. It is known that the Chernobyl accident in 1986 had a dramatic impact on the debate and injected new urgency into the process of rethinking the Soviet view of possible future conflict in Europe. It became even clearer that any form of large-scale conflict, conventional or nuclear, would be a complete catastrophe in view of the fragility of modern civilization. Thus, the concepts of reasonable sufficiency and the defensive nature of military strategy became part of the new Warsaw Pact doctrine proclaimed in May 1987. But throughout 1987 the emphasis on counteroffensive persisted in statements by military leaders.

By early 1988, political leaders seemed to have moved further towards adopting a 'defensive defence' position. Central Committee Secretary Anatoly Dobrynin, for example, made explicit reference to the alternative defence concepts developed in the West.[37] Foreign Minister Eduard Shevardnadze made an appeal at the United Nations for member states to change to a defensive strategy and to restructure their military forces for non-offensive defence.[38] In the course of the year, it became evident that the military leadership was giving some ground by emphasizing the new defensive orientation which was to become part of operational planning. It is known that serious work has been done towards devising more defensive military responses. This was demonstrated by a large-scale Warsaw Pact exercise in March 1988 in which new defensive operational principles were reportedly used. As Edward Warner has reported:

> The scenario for this exercise apparently simulated a large-scale NATO invasion of Eastern Europe. The Pact responded with a purely defensive operation, followed by a limited counteroffensive over a three-week period that halted after expelling the NATO forces from Pact territory. Akhromeev asserted that this three-week period would have provided political leaders on both sides ample opportunity to terminate the war. He also indicated that should these peace-making efforts have failed, the USSR would have been prepared to resume its offensive drive westwards to defeat NATO forces.[39]

During a visit to Bonn in 1989 Gareev announced the disbanding of the Operational Manoeuvre Groups which for many Western analysts symbolized the offensive nature of Soviet military strategy. This decision is part of the process whereby the military has sought to accommodate the political pressure for a more defensive orientation while maintaining the capabilities which it perceives as necessary to accomplish its task. The result is an uneasy compromise. The Soviet military has made changes, but the old strategic thinking is clearly still dominant, and most of the offensive capabilities have been retained. From the Western standpoint, however, the unilateral force reductions announced by Gorbachev at the United Nations in December 1988 are a clear sign that he is serious. The resignation of Akhromeev is evidence both of conflict with the military over these issues and of Gorbachev's determination to impose his will. The appointment of the relatively junior Moiseev as Chief of the General Staff is an indication of its downgrading in the defence policy-making apparatus.

It is worth recalling Gorbachev's statement at the United Nations:

We are witnessing the emergence of a new historic reality – a turning away from the principle of superarmament to the principle of reasonable defence sufficiency. We are present at the birth of a new model of ensuring security – not through the build-up of arms, as was almost always the case in the past, but on the contrary, through their reduction on the basis of compromise ... The Soviet Union has taken a decision to reduce its armed forces. Within the next two years their numerical strength will be reduced by 500,000 men. The numbers of conventional armaments will also be substantially reduced. This will be done unilaterally ... We have decided to withdraw by 1991 six tank divisions from the GDR, Czechoslovakia and Hungary, and to disband them. Assault landing troops and several other formations and units, including assault crossing units with their weapons and combat equipment, will also be withdrawn from the groups of Soviet forces stationed in those countries. Soviet forces stationed in those countries will be reduced by 50,000 men, and their armament by 5,000 tanks. All Soviet divisions remaining, for the time being, in the territory of our allies are being reorganized. *Their structure will be different from what it is now; after a major cutback of their tanks it will become clearly defensive.* At the same time, we shall reduce the numerical strength of the armed forces and the numbers of armaments stationed in the European part of the USSR. In total, Soviet armed forces in this part of our country and in the territories of our European allies will be reduced by 10,000 tanks, 8,500 artillery systems and 800 combat aircraft.[40] [Emphasis added]

What will be the precise impact of these unilateral reductions on the balance of forces on the Central Front is a very complicated issue. Given the varying quality of the forces (in particular the tanks), precise information and detailed analysis are required. Most commentators tend to agree, however, that the reduction in forward-deployed tank forces is substantial and the impact on the position on the Central Front not just symbolic. Some Western observers take the view that the unilateral reductions have seriously diminished the Soviet capability for a large-scale 'standing start' attack on Western Europe.[41] It is of great significance that the political leadership did back those voices arguing for unilateral measures and a commitment to the restructuring of the Warsaw Pact to achieve a non-offensive orientation. Among the concrete measures involved in the restructuring of forces in Eastern Europe are the withdrawal of paratroop and bridging units, the reduction of the numbers of tanks per tank division from 328 to 260 and the conversion of motorized-rifle divisions in the GDR and Czechoslovakia by removing their tank regiments. Apart from reducing offensive systems, additional defensive measures will be introduced: an increase in anti-tank and air defence systems, and measures to slow down enemy advances by creating obstacles and laying minefields.[42]

These measures have not yet transformed the Soviet military strategy and force posture to one of non-provocative 'defensive defence'. There are some signs, moreover, that academic experts are shifting the emphasis from 'defensive defence' to conventional stability as a more appropriate objective of force restructuring.[43] It is not yet clear where the process of restructuring of the Soviet armed forces will lead or whether the threat posed by Soviet conventional capabilities in Europe can be so far reduced that military confrontation in Central Europe can be relegated to history. But it has had the effect of convincing many sceptics that something serious is happening. It has thus imparted particular momentum to negotiations for conventional force reductions in Europe.

Prospects for conventional arms control

The first effort to engage in conventional arms control on the Central Front in Europe, the so-called Mutual and Balanced Force Reduction negotiations, began in 1973; their 'glacial progress' has become legendary. The main reason for their failure was the divergence between the central objectives of the two sides. The WTO objective was to maintain the existing balance at somewhat reduced levels, whereas the NATO objective was an asymmetrical reduction to correct a perceived Warsaw Treaty Organization superiority. An associated difficulty was the 'data issue', an unresolved disagreement about the actual level of existing forces. The issue of verification was another important stumbling-block, as the WTO was not willing to accept the kind of intrusive verification procedures which NATO believed were necessary.

Paradoxically, part of the problem was that the political objectives which East and West were pursuing in the negotiations were achieved (at least in part) without much progress in the negotiations themselves. The WTO managed to get the CSCE process established, while the West Germans successfully pursued their *Ostpolitik*. The MBFR process helped to avert the threat of unilateral force withdrawals by NATO members; domestic pressures in this direction largely explained the American and British interest in MBFR.

The advent of the new thinking and its manifestation in the arms control process has overturned many of the basic assumptions that had made conventional arms control in Europe a hopeless task. The first and perhaps most fundamental factor is the apparent existence of a political will on both sides to achieve substantial results. Since the INF Treaty, strategic arms control has lost some of its political salience and further arms control regimes in theatre nuclear weapons have been made subject to success in at least the first phase of conventional arms control. If the arms control process, which is a centrepiece of Gorbachev's strategy to improve East-West relations, is to progress, then it has to move forward in the conventional sphere. Furthermore, success at the current CFE (Conventional Forces in Europe) talks will legitimize further reductions in Soviet conventional forces which appear to be inevitable for domestic reasons. In the West, the talks have generated much optimism and there is a great deal of political pressure for progress.

Second, the fundamental premise on which the Warsaw Pact approached conventional arms control in the past, namely, that its purpose was to legitimize and thus perpetuate the status quo, has been discarded. The acceptance by the Soviet leadership of the need for asymmetrical reductions has made 'equality of outcome' the fundamental principle, in Lawrence Freedman's terms, not 'equality of sacrifice'.[44]

Third, in January 1989 the extension of glasnost to the military sphere resulted in the USSR publishing figures on the military balance in Central Europe which could be taken seriously. While still disputed by NATO experts, the new statistics at least did not try to claim equality in the same way as those presented in the MBFR period.[45] This means that there is good reason to believe that the data issue can be resolved.

Finally, the Warsaw Pact appeared ready to accept the intrusive verification measures required. Experience of the implementation of the measures agreed at the Conference on Confidence- and Security-Building Measures and Disarmament in Europe in Stockholm in

Conventional force planning

1986 and the INF Treaty in December 1987 has shown that the Soviets are indeed willing to comply with the verification regimes.

During a visit to East Germany on 18 April 1986 Gorbachev proposed the reduction of conventional forces in Europe 'from the Atlantic to the Urals', a proposal which was elaborated in the 'Budapest Appeal' of the Political Consultative Committee of the WTO on 11 July 1986. The principle of negotiations about force reductions in the area 'from the Atlantic to the Urals' was accepted by the Western alliance and by early 1989 a mandate had been agreed upon, mostly on Western terms, for negotiations on conventional forces in Europe. It was subsequently given strong political momentum by President Bush, who set an ambitious timetable and partially conceded a key Warsaw Pact demand for the inclusion of helicopters and land-based combat aircraft. The objective is to reach agreement on the first phase by 1990 and to implement it by 1992. The primary emphasis of the NATO proposals has been on reducing equipment, in particular tanks, to a level as much as 15% below NATO's current levels on the basis of parity. Manpower ceilings for American and Soviet troops deployed in Central Europe are to be reduced according to the same principle to 10% below NATO's current levels, with ceilings for individual European states to be agreed. The Soviet Union proposed a three-phase plan, the first phase from 1991 to 1994, the second from 1994 to 1997 and the third from 1997 to 2000. The first phase would have the same framework as the discussions currently taking place, the second phase would involve further cuts by 25% of manpower and armaments. The third phase would involve the restructuring of the armed forces on both sides according to strictly non-offensive principles.[46]

Any detailed look at the precise numbers and categories of equipment involved will immediately reveal numerous areas of disagreement and difficulties posed by the extraordinary complexity of the issues involved. Nevertheless, it is currently assumed that there is sufficient political will and indeed pressure for success to allow this obstacle to be overcome. One can certainly be optimistic about the first phase. The second phase presents a much greater challenge, because in the view of many Western military experts any strategy of forward defence would be seriously impaired at lower levels.[47] There is much scope within the first phase of CFE for reducing fears of conventional aggression in Europe. Certain characteristics of the current force deployments in Central Europe are considered by both sides as inherently highly destabilizing. The rapid political changes occurring in Eastern Europe, including the Soviet Union, will of course alter the political context of arms control even during the first phase. Any further force reductions – which may lead to quite substantial demilitarization – will take place in a completely different political climate.

8
THE FUTURE OF EAST-WEST RELATIONS

The rapid political changes in Eastern Europe and the Soviet Union have given rise to a widespread perception that we are now in a period of transition from a bipolar system of international relations to a multipolar system. On the one hand, this has given rise to a great deal of euphoria based on the prospect that the East-West antagonism of the last four decades is finally at an end. On the other hand, there is a great deal of anxiety about the shift from a highly stable bipolar configuration to an unknown situation that might prove unstable; even if it ultimately proves possible to achieve an alternative stable security system, the process of transition might be very turbulent and dangerous.

Such pessimism is not entirely without foundation. While Gorbachev has managed to consolidate his control over the political system, including the defence policy agenda, the economic decline of the Soviet Union has proved serious enough to make the failure of perestroika a grim possibility. Even in the major cities of the USSR shortages of basic goods have pushed public discontent to new heights and Gorbachev's popularity is on the wane. While Western Europe moves towards closer integration, Eastern Europe is disintegrating. The Brezhnev doctrine has been repudiated by the Soviet Union. In Poland the Communist Party is no longer in power, there is open speculation about Hungary's departure from the WTO, and the authority of the East German regime collapsed as tens of thousands of its citizens left the country, resulting in the pulling down of the Berlin Wall and the process of German reunification

The future of East-West relations

which is now under way. The internal security of the Soviet Union itself is threatened by the growing political assertiveness of nationalists in the republics.

Although the old bipolar system provided stability for a considerable period, Soviet analysts are correct in perceiving a bipolar system based on long-term military competition to be unstable in the long term. While superpower rivalry and the threat of nuclear war may have imposed a certain discipline on the members of the opposing alliances, a fundamental antagonism of this sort cannot be held in check indefinitely. From the economic perspective alone, it is perfectly clear that the spiralling cost of new generations of increasingly sophisticated conventional and nuclear weapons technologies must eventually become unsustainable for at least one of the protagonists. While for the West the economic crunch is still distant, the political burdens of East-West rivalry have become unbearable, particularly in West Germany, which is at the dividing line between East and West. New thinking, then, simply recognizes the necessity of devising the means for making a cooperative transition to a new and stable security regime.

The military component of East-West relations will be reduced in importance, and the political and economic aspects will be concomitantly more significant. Given the growing economic disparity between Eastern and Western Europe, any cooperative security system in Europe must involve substantial economic help from the West. This is one of the most difficult aspects of the entire situation, as there is no clear conception of how economic reform can be made to work effectively in the East European countries even with substantial Western help.

The military factor, with which this book has been concerned, remains of great importance nevertheless. There is a peculiar dialectic between military power and political intentions. Even very substantial military power is not necessarily perceived as threatening if political relations between states are friendly. Yet the deep antagonism between East and West in the postwar era means that even at a time of much improved relations and close East-West cooperation a large degree of ambiguity about political intentions will remain so long as the process of political reform is incomplete. One case in point is the way the Soviet military continues in many of its traditional modes of thinking, even though it has been forced to accept a radical revision in military doctrine by the political leaders.

In this situation the presence of a large offensive military potential continues to cause anxiety, particularly when Eastern Europe has so many sources of political instability.

For this reason, should a cooperative transition to an alternative security regime in Europe prove to be a real possibility, a substantial change in the military landscape would not be a sufficient condition for its success. It would, however, be a necessary condition and it is therefore useful to summarize some of the elements of such a change.

Minimum nuclear deterrence

The intense controversies over nuclear deterrence in East and West over the last decade have shown that there are no clear answers to the dilemmas posed by the existence of nuclear weapons. The search for unilateral solutions to the security problems have proved fruitless. The endless debates and technical solutions to the dilemma of extended deterrence have only shown that it is ultimately impossible to resolve. Nevertheless, they have also shown that the central nuclear stalemate and the presence of nuclear weapons in Europe are important factors making war in Europe an unacceptable option for everyone. The problem has been that the competitive deployment of nuclear weapons and the strategic debate that accompanies it have proved politically too burdensome and indeed destabilizing.

The Gorbachev era has seen another phenomenon, namely a commitment to complete nuclear disarmament accompanied by wide-ranging arms control offers resulting in the large-scale reduction of nuclear weapons deployed in Europe. The denuclearization of Europe has been viewed with varying degrees of alarm by European leaders because the resulting enhancement of the Soviet conventional threat might allow the USSR to exercise a powerful political influence over Western Europe in the future.

There are signs, however, that the Gorbachev regime and its advisers in the academic institutes are coming to terms with the notion of establishing a regime where a minimum level of strategic and tactical nuclear forces is maintained. Despite some political pressure for movement towards a 'third zero', it now seems that the denuclearization programmes will come to an end. There now exists a great deal of political will to use the START framework to create a stable regime of central strategic nuclear deterrence at a much reduced level. Although there are still many pitfalls, as we have seen, it is imperative that the opportunities that now exist should be made use of. For Britain this means that the role of its strategic nuclear forces and their place in the arms control regime will need fundamental revision in a post-START environment, particularly if current efforts for a de-MIRVed strategic force posture on both sides are successful. With regard to tactical nuclear forces, we are nowhere near either to developing a strategic rationale for their presence other than fear of theatre denuclearization, or to defining the characteristics of tactical systems which could contribute to stability in Central Europe. Unilateral modernization by the West, particularly of air-launched systems, could be very harmful to the entire process of negotiating a stable nuclear balance.

Towards conventional stability in Europe
Conventional force reductions are an essential element of the process of orderly change in Europe. The dramatic shifts in Soviet military doctrine, the recognition of asymmetries on the central front and the unilateral force reductions have gone some way towards giving credence to the notion that the Soviet leadership is serious about dealing with the security problem in Central Europe. Soviet specialists now seem aware that the search for purely defensive force postures may not be the most fruitful way to proceed. Since military capabilities are a reflection of an underlying political conflict, it may not be possible to devise force postures that can be guaranteed not to become an instrument in such a conflict while still providing adequate security. The process of democratization in the Soviet Union and the movement away from communism in Eastern Europe are widely seen as removing the ideological basis for the fundamental antagonism between East and West. This constitutes the most significant factor in dispelling perceptions of a threat. While it is not clear whether there can be a purely defensive force posture, it is also evident, however, that certain weapons deployment modes (e.g. large tank formations) which are obviously very suitable for an offensive role can be replaced by others which are more defensive (e.g. anti-tank weapons). The elimination of major conventional imbalances, the decrease in surprise attack capabilities and a shift towards a more obviously defensive force posture should be within reach of the CFE process in the foreseeable future.

The future of East-West relations

The paradox of the current situation is that as the military threat in Europe decreases, the rapid political changes have introduced new and perhaps more imminent dangers. Arms control continues to play a role in reducing the military threat, and it is important that of all the various configurations of future arms control agreements the West pursues those which lead to the most stable security regimes. The pulling down of the Berlin Wall and the process of German reunification have profound consequences for NATO and the Warsaw Pact. In the long term, nothing less than a formal settlement of the East-West conflict, involving new forms of political and economic relationships between East and West, with a united Germany at the centre and an institutional mechanism for the regulation of European security, will be able to meet the challenges that are ahead.

NOTES

Chapter 1
1. Daniel Yergin, *Shattered Peace* (Harmondsworth: Penguin, 1977), p. 11.
2. Ibid.
3. For an instructive example of this way of thinking, consider the shifts in the West German Chancellor Adenauer's view of 'peaceful coexistence' in the aftermath of the intervention in Hungary in 1956 as documented in Peter Siebenmorgen, *Gezeitenwechsel* (Bonn: Bouvier Verlag, 1990).
4. See Hans Wassmund, *Kontinuität im Wandel* (Cologne: Bohlau Verlag, 1974); Yergin, op. cit.; for a more recent exposition of this view, see Jonathan Steele, *The Limits of Soviet Power* (Harmondsworth: Penguin, 1983); Fred Halliday, *The Making of the Second Cold War* (London: Verso, 1983).
5. See, for example, Marie Mendras, 'Policy outside and politics inside' in Archie Brown (ed.), *Political Leadership in the Soviet Union* (London: Macmillan, 1989), pp. 127–62.
6. Harriet Fast Scott and William F. Scott, *Soviet Military Doctrine* (Boulder, CO: Westview Press, 1988), p. 264.
7. See Gerhard Wettig, 'Comments on the paper of Lawrence Freedman', in Murray Feshbach (ed.), *National Security Issues of the USSR* (Dordrecht: Martinus Nijhoff Publishers, 1987), pp. 91–7; Wettig evidently could not make up his mind whether the Soviets wanted an INF agreement or not. In either case their preference would be based, in his view, on hostile intentions.
8. Michael MccGwire, *Military Objectives in Soviet Foreign Policy* (Washington, DC: Brookings Institution, 1987).

Notes

9 Stephen Sestanovich, 'Gorbachev's diplomacy of decline', *Problems of Communism*, January/February 1988, pp. 1–15.
10 Stephen Shenfield, *The Nuclear Predicament* (London: Routledge/ RIIA, 1987); Allen Lynch, *The Soviet Study of International Relations*, (Cambridge: Cambridge University Press, 1989).

Chapter 2

1 Army General S. Ivanov, 'Soviet military doctrine and strategy', *Voennaya mysl'*, no. 5, May 1969, pp. 40–51; this quotation from p. 46.
2 The achievement of nuclear parity was accompanied in Soviet military thought with a recognition of the mutual vulnerability of the superpowers and thus the reduced likelihood of nuclear escalation by either side. See Ivanov, op. cit.
3 For more detailed discussion, see Christoph Bluth, 'The Evolution of Soviet Military Doctrine', *Survival*, vol. XXX, no. 2, pp. 149–62.
4 *Pravda*, 19 January 1977; see also L. I. Brezhnev, *Na strazhe mira i sotsializma* (Moscow: Politizdat, 1979), pp. 491–2; for discussion see Tsuyoshi Hasegawa, 'Soviets on nuclear-war-fighting', *Problems of Communism*, vol. XXXV, no. 4, July-August 1986, pp. 68–79; Robbin F. Laird and Dale R. Herspring, *The Soviet Union and Strategic Arms* (Boulder, CO: Westview Press, 1984), pp. 20–22; Michael MccGwire, *Military Objectives in Soviet Foreign Policy* (Washington, DC: Brookings Institution, 1987), Chapters 2 and 3; David R. Jones, 'Soviet military doctrine and space in the 1980s', in Carl G. Jacobson (ed.), *The Uncertain Course* (Oxford: Oxford University Press (SIPRI), 1987), pp. 93–135.
5 David Holloway, *The Soviet Union and the Arms Race* (New Haven, CT: Yale University Press, 1984), p. 50.
6 *Pravda*, 21 October 1981.
7 Marshal N. V. Ogarkov, *Vsegda v gotovnosti k zashchite otechestva* (Moscow: Voenizdat, 1982).
8 For an analysis of Soviet deep-strike concepts and the employment of Operational Manoeuvre Groups, see Christopher Donnelly, *The Red Banner* (London: Jane's Information Group, 1988), Chapter 13.
9 For a detailed analysis of the Ustinov-Ogarkov debates, see Hasegawa, op. cit. See also MccGwire, op. cit., Chapters 13 and 14. A recent authoritative account of contemporary Soviet military doctrine is given in M. A. Gareev, *M. V. Frunze – voennyi teoretik* (Moscow: Voenizdat, 1985).
10 Cf. MccGwire, op. cit., p. 312, where the documentary evidence is cited.
11 The arguments outlined in this section have been developed in

Notes

considerable detail in Pat Litherland, *Gorbachev and Arms Control: Civilian Experts and Soviet Policy*, Peace Research Report Number 12 (Bradford: Bradford University School of Peace Studies, 1986); Stephen Shenfield, *The Nuclear Predicament* (London: Routledge/RIIA, 1987); A. Bovin, *Izvestiya*, 20 October 1979.

12 Genrikh Trofimenko, *The U. S. Military Doctrine* (Moscow: Progress Publishers, 1986). On p. 210 Trofimenko quotes Mikhail Gorbachev as saying: 'Diminished security of the United States of America as compared to that of the Soviet Union would not be to our advantage, for that would lead to mistrust and instability.' For further reference to Trofimenko's views, see Litherland, op. cit., p. 63.

13 V. M. Gavrilov and S. V. Patrushev, 'Gonka vooruzhenii v ierarkhii global'nykh problem', *Voprosy filosofii*, no. 5, 1984, pp. 99–107; A. G. Arbatov, 'Voenno-strategicheskoe ravnovesie i politika administratsii Reigana', *MEMO*, no. 10, 1984, pp. 3–14; and A. G. Arbatov, *Voenno-strategicheskii paritet i politika SShA* (Moscow: Politizdat, 1984). An updated version of this book has been published in English as Aleksei G. Arbatov, *Lethal Frontiers* (New York: Praeger, 1988). For a very subtle analysis of the article by Gavrilov and Patrushev, see Litherland, op. cit., pp. 66f.

14 See Shenfield, op. cit., p. 87.

15 For an assessment of the influence of 'new thinking' on the Soviet leadership, and the continuing influence of 'old thinking', see ibid.; the view held by all the academics I interviewed at IMEMO, ISKAN and the Institute of Europe is that the military leadership is still dominated by the 'old thinking', with some exceptional figures such as General Chaldymov who are at least willing to listen to new ideas.

16 M. A. Gareev, *M. V. Frunze – Military Theorist* (London: Pergamon-Brassey's, 1988), p. 216.

17 Ibid.

18 Ibid., p. 385.

19 One leading academic, for example, has warned that his writings should not be over-interpreted and that reasonable sufficiency is not in itself a concept that can be made operational. Personal conversation with the author, 3 November 1988.

20 L. Semeyko, 'Vmesto gor oruzhiya – o printsipe dostatochnosti', *Izvestiya*, 13 August 1987, p. 5.

21 These debates will be covered in some more detail in a later chapter.

22 Raymond L. Garthoff, 'New Thinking in Soviet Military Doctrine', *The Washington Quarterly*, Summer 1988, pp. 131–58; this quotation from p. 136; compare this with the definition of Soviet military doctrine given at the beginning of this chapter.

23 Makhmut Gareev, 'Soviet military doctrine: current and future developments', *RUSI Journal*, vol. 133, no. 4, Winter 1988, pp. 5–10.
24 For the clearest Soviet statement on deterrence, see Aleksei Arbatov, 'Parity and Reasonable Sufficiency', *International Affairs* (Moscow), October 1988, pp. 75–87, and Arbatov, 1988, op. cit.

Chapter 3

1 For an example of this kind of argument, see Robert Slusser, *The Berlin Crisis of 1961* (Baltimore: Johns Hopkins Press, 1973).
2 For a forceful exposition of this point of view, see Seweryn Bialer, ' "New thinking" and Soviet foreign policy', *Survival*, vol. XXX, no. 4, July/August 1988, pp. 291–309.
3 For a Soviet account of the problems of the Soviet economy and the strategy of the Gorbachev leadership to deal with them, see Abel Aganbegyan, *The Challenge: Economics of Perestroika* (London: Hutchinson, 1988); for a perceptive analysis of the structural problems of the Soviet economy and its relation to security policy, see James Sherr, *Soviet Power: The Continuing Challenge* (London: Macmillan/RUSI, 1987), Chapter 2.
4 Bialer, op. cit., p. 292.
5 Arthur J. Alexander, *Decision-Making in Soviet Weapons Procurement*, Adelphi Paper No. 147/148, (London: IISS, 1978), p. 5.
6 See David Holloway, *The Soviet Union and the Arms Race* (New Haven, CT: Yale University Press, 1984), p. 109.
7 Alexander, op. cit., p. 15.
8 Roman Kolkowicz, *The Soviet Military and the Communist Party* (Princeton, NJ: Princeton University Press, 1967); Malcolm Mackintosh, 'The Soviet military – influence on foreign policy', *Problems of Communism*, September-October 1976, pp. 1–12; William E. Odom, 'The party connection', *Problems of Communism*, September-October 1976, pp. 12–16.
9 Viktor G. Kulikov, *Pravda*, 13 November 1974, quoted in translation from Kenneth Currie, 'Soviet General Staff's new role', *Problems of Communism*, March-April 1984, pp. 32–40; this quotation from p. 35.
10 Alexander O. Ghebhardt, 'Implications for organizational bureaucratic policy models for Soviet ABM decisionmaking', unpublished Ph.D. dissertation, Columbia University, 1975, p. 66.
11 Condoleezza Rice, 'The party, the military and decision authority in the Soviet Union', *World Politics*, vol. XL, no. 1, October 1987, pp. 55–81.
12 For more detail on the various institutes, their history and their role

Notes

in the Soviet political process, see Oded Eran, *Mezhdunarodniki* (Ramat Gan, Israel: Turtledove Publishing, 1979).

13 See Allen Lynch, *The Soviet Study of International Relations* (Cambridge: Cambridge University Press, 1989).

14 F. Stephen Larrabee, 'Gorbachev and the Soviet military', *Foreign Affairs*, vol. 66, no. 5, Summer 1988, pp. 1002–26; this reference to p. 1018.

15 Malcolm Mackintosh, 'Changes in the Soviet High Command under Gorbachev', *RUSI Journal*, vol. 133, no. 1, Spring 1988, pp. 49–56; this quotation from p. 51.

16 Maj. Gen. V. Fedorov, Col. E. Zabavin, Col. V. Podolety, 'Perestroika i demokratizatsiya nashei armeiskoi zhizni', *Kommunist vooruzhennykh sil*, no. 16, August 1987, pp. 9–16; 'Armiya v usloviyakh demokratizatsii', *Kommunist*, no. 14, September 1987, pp.117–19; for discussion see an unpublished paper by Stephen Dalziel, 'Perestroyka, glasnost' and the Soviet military', presented at the NASEES Annual Conference, Cambridge, 26–8 March 1988; Marion Recktenwald, *Perestrojka in den sowjetischen Streitkräften* (Cologne: Berichte des Bundesinstituts für ostwissenschaftliche und internationale Studien, 1988).

17 One of the important appointments, as Malcolm Mackintosh has pointed out (op. cit.), was the promotion of Yazov protégé Vladimir Lobov to First Deputy Chief of the General Staff in March 1987.

18 *Pravda*, 28 January 1987.

19 Dale R. Herspring, 'On perestroyka: Gorbachev, Yazov, and the military', *Problems of Communism*, July-August 1987, vol. XXXVI, July-August 1987, pp. 99–107; this quotation from p. 103.

20 Aleksei Izyumov, 'Military glasnost lacks openness', *Moscow News*, no. 37, 1989, p. 4.

21 *Soviet Weekly*, 6 August 1988, p. 4.

22 Julian Cooper, 'Nuclear milking machines and perestroika', *Detente*, no. 14, 1989, pp. 11–13; this quotation from p. 12.

23 Dale R. Herspring, 'The Soviet military and change', *Survival*, vol. XXXI, no. 4, July/August 1989, pp. 321–338; this reference to p. 327.

24 Aleksei I. Izyumov, 'The demilitarization of the Soviet economy', *Telos*, Fall 1989, pp. 11–14; this reference to p. 13; one such sale of military equipment took place at the Exhibition for Economic Achievements (VDNKh) while the author was in Moscow in December 1989.

Chapter 4

1 Robert P. Berman and John C. Baker, *Soviet Strategic Forces*, (Washington, DC: Brookings Institution, 1982); Christoph Bluth,

Notes

'Defence and security' in Martin McCauley (ed.), *Khrushchev and Khrushchevism* (London: Macmillan, 1987), pp. 194–214.

2. International Institute for Strategic Studies, *The Military Balance 1988–89* (London: Jane's Defence Publishers, 1988); see also Berman and Baker, op. cit., p. 105.

3. Robbin F. Laird and Dale R. Herspring, *The Soviet Union and Strategic Arms* (Boulder, CO: Westview Press, 1984).

4. See Berman and Baker, op. cit., Chapter 3 and Appendix B; Donald MacKenzie, 'The Soviet Union and strategic missile guidance', *International Security*, vol. 13, no. 2, Fall 1988, pp. 5–54. This section is also based on a conversation with Stephen Meyer at MIT, Cambridge, MA, in May 1988.

5. Analysts distinguish between counterforce, countermilitary and countervalue targets. These refer respectively to the enemy strike forces (in particular nuclear missiles and aircraft), military installations and equipment, and civilian targets (cities, industrial centres).

6. See Laird and Herspring, op. cit.; see also Michael MccGwire, *Military Objectives in Soviet Foreign Policy* (Washington, DC: The Brookings Institution, 1987), Appendix D.

7. IISS, op. cit.

8. In the late 1970s and early 1980s there was a widespread view among certain US political circles that the Soviet Union was seeking complete strategic nuclear superiority over the United States, to be used either in political blackmail or else to actually engage in strategic nuclear conflict – hence the emphasis on ICBMs. Such arguments were used to support political opposition to the SALT II agreement by a group of politicians and experts called the Committee on the Present Danger. See Robert Scheer, *With Enough Shovels: Reagan, Bush and Nuclear War* (London: Secker & Warburg, 1982), Chapter 4 for more details.

9. Berman and Baker, op. cit., pp. 106 f.; Laird and Herspring, op. cit., pp. 55–8.

10. For a detailed examination of this proposal, see Stephen Shenfield, 'Entering the third millennium nuclear-free: reflections on the Soviet proposal to eliminate nuclear weapons by the Year 2000', Paper presented at a meeting of the British International Studies Association, King's College, London, 17 July 1987.

11. See Committee of Soviet Scientists for Peace Against the Nuclear Threat, *Strategic Stability under the Conditions of Radical Nuclear Arms Reductions* (Moscow: Novosti, 1987); Aleksei Arbatov, 'Strategic equilibrium and stability', in Evgeny Primakov (ed.), *Disarmament and Security 1987 Yearbook* (Moscow: Novosti, 1988), pp. 239–63.

12 Arbatov, in Primakov, op. cit., p. 255.
13 Ibid., p. 248.
14 Aleksei Arbatov, 'How much defence is enough?', *International Affairs* (Moscow), April 1989, pp. 31–44.
15 See, for example, A. P. Vasil'ev and V. K. Rudyuk, 'Dostatochna li protivovozdushnaya oborona?', *Voennaya mysl'*, no. 9, 1989, pp. 59–68.
16 Sergei Vybornov, Andrei Gusenkov and Vladimir Leontiev, 'Nothing is simple in Europe', *International Affairs* (Moscow), March 1988, pp. 34–41; for a reply, see Vladimir Stupishin, 'Indeed, nothing in Europe is simple', *International Affairs* (Moscow), May 1988, pp. 69–71; for a more extensive discussion of recent ideas about 'minimum nuclear deterrence' proposed by Soviet specialists see Stephen Shenfield, *Minimum Nuclear Deterrence: the Debate among Soviet Civilian Analysts* (Rhode Island: Brown University, 1989).
17 Michele A. Flournoy, 'START cutting Soviet strategic forces', *Arms Control Today*, June/July 1989, pp. 15–21.
18 Robert Einhorn, 'Strategic arms reduction talks', *Survival*, vol. XXX, no. 5, September/October 1988, pp. 387–99; Walter B. Slocombe, 'Force posture consequences of the START treaty', *Survival*, vol. XXX, no. 5, September/October 1988, pp. 402–7.
19 Academic experts from IMEMO are convinced that economic constraints will prevent a significant expansion of Soviet strategic bomber capabilities. (Interviews in Moscow, December 1989.)

Chapter 5

1 Alexander O. Ghebhardt, 'Implications of organizational and bureaucratic policy models for Soviet ABM decisionmaking', unpublished Ph.D. dissertation, Columbia University, 1975, Chapter I; P. F. Batitsky, 'Voiska protivovozdushnoi oborony strany', *Voenno-istoricheskii zhurnal*, no. 8, 1967, p. 26; P. F. Batitsky, *Voiska protivovozdushnoi oborony strany*, Part III (Moscow: Voenizdat, 1968), p. 341.
2 Ghebhardt, op. cit., p. 14.
3 Lawrence Freedman, *US Intelligence and the Soviet Strategic Threat* (London: Macmillan, 1977), p. 87.
4 *Pravda*, 25 October 1961, p. 5.
5 *New York Times*, 17 July 1962, p. 1.
6 See for example the article by Cols I. Zheltikov and V. Igolkin, 'Certain tendencies in the development of antiaircraft and antirocket defenses', *Voennaya mysl'*, no. 8, 1964, pp. 53–65.
7 *Pravda*, 3 April 1966, p. 3; M. V. Zakharov, *Tekhnika i vooruzhenie*, no. 4, April 1966, p. 8.

8. An indication that these problems were exercising the minds of the Soviet military could be found in an article by Major-General I. Anureev which contained an analytical model of the correlation of forces. The probability coefficient for overcoming anti-air defence was given as 0.7 (assuming a kill ratio of 30%), while the probability for overcoming anti-missile defence was assumed to be 1. Although Anureev described the given values as purely hypothetical, some conclusion about what these values were likely to be would seem to be warranted. Major-General I. Anureev, 'Determining the correlation of forces in terms of nuclear weapons', *Voennaya mysl'*, no. 6, June 1967, p. 38; for a discussion of later elaborations of Anureev's model, see Stephen M. Meyer, 'Soviet strategic programmes and the US SDI', *Survival*, vol. XXVII, no. 6, November/December 1985, pp. 274–92; about the disappearance of ABMs from public parades, see Michael Rühle, *Die Strategische Verteidigung in Rüstung und Politik der UdSSSR* (Cologne: Bundesinstitut für ostwissenschaftliche und internationale Studien, 1985), p. 7.

9. Raymond L. Garthoff, 'BMD and East-West relations', in Ashton B. Carter and David N. Schwartz, (eds), *Ballistic Missile Defence* (Washington, DC: Brookings Institution, 1984), pp. 275–319; this quotation from p. 302.

10. In the internal British debate about the future of the independent nuclear deterrent, a consensus developed in Whitehall that a capability to attack Moscow was essential. This meant that British strategic nuclear forces had to be capable of penetrating strategic defences in the Moscow area. This requirement has become known as the 'Moscow criterion'. See Christoph Bluth, 'The Security Dimension', in Alex Pravda and Peter J. S. Duncan (eds), *Soviet-British Relations since the 1970s* (Cambridge: Cambridge University Press for RIIA, 1990), pp. 92–119.

11. David S. Yost, 'Soviet ballistic missile defense and NATO', *Orbis*, vol. 29, no. 2, Summer 1985, pp. 281–92; this reference to p. 284. Apparently it has been successfully tested against the Soviet Scaleboard missile.

12. Ibid., p. 283.

13. Soviet laser systems have been credited with the capability of interfering with the sensors of US satellites. Certainly the Soviets have not deployed or tested any laser systems capable of destroying satellites or missiles.

14. Quoted in translation from Aleksei G. Arbatov, *Lethal Frontiers* (New York: Praeger, 1988), p. 183.

15. Karen Puschel, 'Can Moscow live with SDI?', *Survival*, vol. XXXI,

no. 1, January/February 1989, pp. 34–51; this reference to p. 39. The section here is to some extent based on this article.
16. Generally speaking, in arms control it has been possible to trade restraints on one system for restraints on equivalent or similar systems. Gorbachev was offering not merely restraint on Soviet BMD, but a whole range of other concessions on arms control in return for a restraint on SDI. Moreover, Soviet understatement of their own BMD research strengthened the American position further.

Chapter 6

1. See Christoph Bluth, 'Defence and Security', in Martin McCauley (ed.), *Khrushchev and Khrushchevism* (London: Macmillan, 1987), pp. 194–214.
2. See David Holloway, 'The INF policy of the Soviet Union', in Hans Henrik Holm and Nikolaj Peterson (eds), *The European Missile Crisis* (London: Frances Pinter, 1983), pp. 92–114; Michael MccGwire, *Military Objectives in Soviet Foreign Policy* (Washington: Brookings Institution, 1987), Appendix D. American success in having Soviet medium-range systems such as the SS-11 and the Backfire counted as strategic compared with the Soviet failure to have American INF counted as such is remarkable (particularly in the Backfire case).
3. Genrikh Trofimenko, *The U.S. Military Doctrine* (Moscow: Progress Publishers, 1986), p. 154.
4. Ibid., p. 159.
5. Quoted from William V. Garner, *Soviet Threat Perceptions of NATO's Eurostrategic Missiles* (Paris: Atlantic Institute of International Affairs, 1983), p. 14.
6. Raymond L. Garthoff, quoted in MccGwire, op. cit., p. 506.
7. Jane M. O. Sharp, 'After Reykjavik: arms control and the Allies', *International Affairs*, vol. 63, no. 2, Spring 1987, pp. 239–57, especially pp. 249–51.
8. See Thomas Risse-Kappen, *The Zero Option* (Boulder, CO: Westview Press, 1988), p. 111.
9. Shevardnadze's speech at the CPSU Congress, 28 February 1986; see Risse-Kappen, op. cit., p. 110.
10. Soviet TV 0700 GMT 9 February, SWB/SU/0072 C/4.
11. See Gerhard Wettig, 'Comments on the Paper of Lawrence Freedman' in Murray Feshbach (ed.), *National Security Issues of the USSR* (Dordrecht: Martinus Nijhoff Publishers, 1987), pp. 91–7 for a critical interpretation of INF.

Notes

12 Uwe Nerlich, 'Der Bedeutungswandel der französischen Nuklearstreitmacht', in Karl Kaiser and Pierre Lellouche (eds), *Deutsch-Französische Sicherheitspolitik* (Bonn: Europa Union Verlag, 1986), p. 179.
13 See Christoph Bluth, 'The Evolution of Soviet Military Doctrine', *Survival*, vol. XXX, no. 2, March/April 1988, pp. 149–61; Michael MccGwire, op. cit.; for Soviet sources on these developments, see M. A. Gareev, *M. V. Frunze – voennyi teoretik* (Moscow: Voenizdat, 1985); M. A. Gareev, *Sovetskaya voennaya nauka* (Moscow: Znanie, 1987); V. V. Larionov et al., *Evolyutsiya voennogo iskusstva: etapy, tendentsii, printsipy* (Moscow: Voenizdat, 1987).
14 Uwe Nerlich, 'Missile defences: strategic and tactical', *Survival*, vol. 27, no. 3 (1985), pp. 119–27; this quotation from p. 121.
15 Helga Haftendorn, 'Transatlantische Dissonanzen. Der Bericht über "Selektive Abschreckung" und die Strategiediskussion in den USA', *Europa-Archiv*, Folge 8, pp. 213–22. See also the article by Egon Bahr, '60 Millionen wiegen schwerer', *Der Spiegel*, 29 February 1988, p. 30.
16 For more detail, see *Der Spiegel*, 29 February 1988, pp. 25–32; Karl-Heinz Kamp, 'Die Modernisierung der nuklearen Kurzstreckenwaffen in Europa', *Europa-Archiv*, vol. 43, no. 10 (1988), pp. 269–76.
17 Denis Healey, *The Time of My Life* (London: Michael Joseph, 1989), p. 243.
18 Anthony Sivers, *Conventional Arms Control: Considering New Directions*, Faraday Discussion Paper no. 13 (London: Brassey's Defence Publishers for the Council for Arms Control, 1989), p. 55.
19 Based on interviews with leading Soviet academics conducted in London and Moscow.

Chapter 7

1 *Pravda*, 17 March 1982.
2 Stephen M. Meyer, 'The sources and prospect of Gorbachev's new political thinking on security', *International Security*, vol. 13, no. 2, Fall 1988, pp. 124–63; this quotation from p. 144.
3 Aleksei Arbatov, 'Parity and reasonable sufficiency', *International Affairs* (Moscow), October 1988, pp. 75–87; this quotation from p. 76.
4 V. V. Zhurkin, S. A. Karaganov and A. V. Kortunov, 'O razumnoi dostatochnosti', *SShA*, no. 12, 1987, pp. 11–21. Vitaly Zhurkin is the Director of the Institute of Europe in Moscow; Sergei Karaganov is the Deputy Director. A. Kortunov is at ISKAN. All

three belong to the group of civilian academics who have long been involved in studies of arms control and disarmament issues. The author benefited from conversations with Dr Karaganov during his visit to King's College, London, in November 1989. For an extended version of their arguments, see V. V. Zhurkin, S. A. Karaganov and A. V. Kortunov, *Razumnaya dostatochnost' i novoe politicheskoe myshlenie* (Moscow: Nauka, 1989). The example is somewhat disingenuous since the Soviet Union did not match American strategic power even by means of ICBMs for quite a long time.

5 *Pravda*, 27 July 1987.
6 S. Akhromeev, 'Doktrina predotvrashcheniya voiny, zashchity mira i sotsializma', *Problemy mira i sotsializma*, no. 12, 1987, pp. 25–7.
7 Editorial, 'Oboronitel'nyi kharakter sovetskoi voennoi doktriny i podgotovka voisk (sil)', *Voennaya mysl'*, no. 1, 1988, pp. 4–13.
8 Editorial, 'Oktyabr' i novoe politicheskoe myshlenie', *Zarubezhnoe voennoe obozrenie*, no. 10, 1988, pp. 3–6.
9 Interview with General of the Army A. I. Gribkov, *Krasnaya zvezda*, 26 November 1987; Admiral Kostev, *Krasnaya zvezda*, 26 November 1987.
10 V. G. Kulikov, 'O voenno-strategicheskom paritete i dostatochnosti dlya oborony', *Voennaya mysl'*, no. 5, 1988, pp. 3–11; this reference to p. 10.
11 Ivan Tret'yak, 'Reliable defence first and foremost', *Moscow News*, 21 February 1988, p. 12.
12 Lt. Gen. V. Serebryannikov, 'Sootnoshenie politcheskikh i voennykh sredstv v zashchite sotsializma', *Kommunist vooruzhennykh sil*, no. 18, September 1987, pp. 9–16; this quotation from p. 15.
13 V. V. Serebryannikov, 'Dialektika politicheskikh i voennykh sredstv v zashchite sotsializma', *Voennaya mysl'*, no. 10, 1988, pp. 3–11.
14 Based on interviews conducted in Moscow, December 1989.
15 G. I. Salmanov, 'Sovetskaya voennaya doktrina i nekotorye vzglyady na kharakter voiny v zashchitu sotsializma', *Voennaya mysl'*, no. 12, 1988, pp. 3–13; see also Kulikov, op. cit.
16 See for example Akhromeev, op. cit.; A. Lizichev, *Trud*, 9 May 1988.
17 D. T. Yazov, *Na strazhe sotsializma i mira* (Moscow: Voenizdat), p. 30; Akhromeev, op. cit. p. 26. These references were drawn to the author's attention in an unpublished paper by Roy Allison.
18 Arbatov, op. cit., p. 82.
19 Aleksei G. Arbatov, *Lethal Frontiers* (New York: Praeger, 1988), pp. 270 f.
20 Viktor G. Kulikov, *Doktrina zashchity mira i sotsializma* (Moscow: Voenizdat, 1988).

21 Pal Dunay has drawn the author's attention to this analysis of the shift to an offensive strategy. See Kulikov, op. cit.; R. A. Savushkin, 'Zarozhdenie i razvitie sovetskoi voennoi doktriny', *Voenno-istoricheskii zhurnal*, February 1988, pp. 19–26; Vladimir N. Lobov, 'Strategiya pobedy', *Voenno-istoricheskii zhurnal*, May 1988; for the relationship between new thinking and Lenin, see Mikhail S. Gorbachev, *Perestroika i novoe myshlenie dlya nashei strany i dlya vsego mira* (Moscow: Voenizdat, 1987), pp. 20 f.
22 See M. A. Gareev, *M. V. Frunze – Military Theorist* (London: Pergamon-Brassey's, 1988), p. 217.
23 See for example Yu. Maksimov, 'Razvitie vzglyadov na oboronu', *Voenno-istoricheskii zhurnal*, October 1979, pp. 10–16; M. M. Kozlov, 'Organizatsiya i vedenie strategicheskoi oborony po opytu Velikoy Otechestvennoi voiny', *Voenno-istoricheskii zhurnal*, December 1980, pp. 9–17; M. M. Kozlov, 'Osobennosti strategicheskoi oborony i kontrnastupleniya i ikh znachenie dlya razvitiya sovetskogo voennogo isskustva', *Voenno-istoricheskii zhurnal*, October 1981, pp. 28–35; G. Ionin, 'Sovremennaya oborona', *Voennyi vestnik*, no. 4, 1981, pp. 15–18; V. Galkin, 'Oboronyaetsya batal'on', *Voennyi vestnik*, no. 3, 1982, pp. 16–19; V. Kravchenko and Yu. Upeniek, 'Vzvod PTUR v oborone', *Voennyi vestnik*, no. 5, 1984, pp. 67–8; V. G. Reznichenko (ed.), *Taktika* (Moscow: Voenizdat, 1984). For discussion see Meyer, op. cit., pp. 153 f; Notra Trulock, Kerry L. Hines and Anne D. Herr, *Soviet Military Thought in Transition: Implications for the Long-Term Military Competition* (Arlington, VA: Pacific-Sierra Corporation, 1988), pp. 104–7.
24 Gareev, op. cit., p. 221.
25 Meyer, op. cit., p. 154.
26 Zhurkin, Karaganov and Kortunov, 1987, op. cit.
27 A. A. Kokoshin, 'Sokrashchenie yadernykh vooruzhenii i strategicheskiya stabil'nost', *SShA*, no. 2, 1988; A. A. Kokoshin, 'Razvitie voennogo dela i sokrashchenie vooruzhennykh sil i obychnykh vooruzhenii', *MEMO*, no. 1, 1988, pp. 20–32.
28 Oleg Amirov, Nikolai Kishilov, Vadim Makarevsky and Yuri Usachev, 'Problems of reducing military confrontation', in Yevgeny Primakov (ed.), *Disarmament and Security 1987 Yearbook* (Moscow: Novosti Press Agency Publishing House for IMEMO, 1988), p. 390.
29 A. Kokoshin and V. Larionov, 'Protivostoyanie sil obshego naznacheniya v kontekste obespecheniya strategicheskoi stabil'nosti', *MEMO*, no. 6, 1988, pp. 24–30.
30 A. A. Kokoshin and A. V. Kortunov, 'Stabil'nost' i peremeny v mezhdunarodnykh otnosheniyakh', *SShA*, no. 7, July 1987, p. 11.

31 A. Kokoshin and V. Larionov, 'Kurskaya bitva v svete sovremennoi oboronitel'noi doktriny', *MEMO*, no. 8, 1987. pp. 32–40.
32 E. F. Ivanovsky, 'Vydayushchayasya pobeda Sovetskoi Armii', *Voenno-istoricheskii zhurnal*, no. 11, November 1987, pp. 44–53.
33 Aleksei Arbatov, 'Military Doctrines', in Primakov, op. cit., p. 200.
34 Vitaly Shlykov, ' "Strong is the armour..." Tank asymmetry and real security', *International Affairs* (Moscow), December 1988, pp. 37–48; this reference to p. 47.
35 See the debate on doctrine between Aleksei Arbatov and V. Serebryannikov in *Novoe vremya*, 1989, nos. 6, 12 and 17.
36 The institutional power of the military is a complex phenomenon. It resides partly in the fact that directives from the political leadership rely for their formulation on expertise supplied by the military, and partly in the fact that general directives are interpreted and implemented by the military bureaucracy in whatever manner is most congenial to their own interests as perceived by their leadership. The military elite, however, also has allies in the Politburo, the Central Committee, the defence industry and other important institutions which may on various issues support them against the General Secretary, for example.
37 *Pravda*, 5 May 1987.
38 *Soviet News*, 15 June 1988, pp. 214–18.
39 Edward L. Warner, 'New thinking and old realities in Soviet defence policy', *Survival*, vol. XXXI, no. 1, January/February 1989, pp. 13–33; this quotation from p. 25. Warner's sources are conversations with US military officers who accompanied Marshal Akhromeev during his visit to the US in July 1988 and reports from Soviet diplomats, who spoke of hearing Akhromeev discuss this same sequence of events in Moscow in summer 1988.
40 Mikhail Gorbachev, Speech to the United Nations General Assembly, 7 December 1988.
41 For a detailed analysis, see Philip A. Karber, *Soviet Implementation of the Gorbachev Unilateral Military Reductions: Implications for Conventional Arms Control in Europe* (BDM Corporation, 14 March 1989); see also Philip A. Karber, 'The military impact of the Gorbachev reductions', *Armed Forces Journal International*, January 1989, p. 64.
42 See Karber, op. cit.; David M. Glantz, 'Soviet Force Structure in an Era of Reform', *The Journal of Soviet Military Studies*, vol. 2, no. 3, September 1989, pp. 361–93; M. Moiseev, 'Sovetskaya voennaya doktrina: realizatsiya oboronitel'noi napravlennosti', *Pravda*, 13 March 1989. I also wish to acknowledge a private communication from Stephen Shenfield.

43 Andrei Kokoshin, Alexander Konovalov, Valentin Larionov and Valeri Mazing, *Problems of Ensuring Stability with Radical Cuts in Armed Forces and Conventional Armaments in Europe* (Moscow: Novosti, 1989).
44 Lawrence Freedman, 'The politics of conventional arms control', *Survival*, vol. XXXI, no. 5, September/October 1989, pp. 387–96.
45 See Lawrence Freedman, 'Moscow enters the numbers game', *The Independent*, 31 January 1989.
46 See Freedman, op. cit.; for more details see Anthony Sivers, *Conventional Arms Control: Considering New Directions*, Faraday Discussion Paper no. 13 (London: Brassey's Defence Publishers for the Council for Arms Control, 1989).
47 See Robert D. Blackwill, 'Conceptual problems of conventional arms control', *International Security*, vol. 12, no. 4, Spring 1988, pp. 28–47.

CHATHAM HOUSE PAPERS

Also in this series

The New Eastern Europe: Western Responses
J. M. C. Rollo

Concentrating on Poland, Hungary, Czechoslovakia and East Germany, this paper looks at the process of moving from a command economy to a market-orientated economy, and reviews the constraints faced by these countries in making such a transition. It was completed only in late March 1990 and was, therefore, at the time of publication, one of the most up-to-date analyses on the market.

Publication: April 1990

Soviet Foreign Policy Priorities under Gorbachev
Alex Pravda

Gorbachev has clearly brought about revolutionary changes in the strategic priorities and methods of Soviet foreign policy. But how deeply rooted are these changes and what do they mean for East-West relations? This paper maps the contours of the 'new' Soviet foreign policy and traces its domestic and international roots.

Publication: late 1990

Soviet Foreign Economic Policy under Perestroika
Leonard Geron

One of the major changes which Gorbachev has made in the Soviet Union is to begin to dismantle the state monopoly of foreign trade. This paper sets current foreign-trade reforms in the wider context of *perestroika* and foreign policy 'new thinking' in the Soviet Union.

Publication: late 1990

RIIA/PINTER PUBLISHERS